# THE EVERYTHING CAKE MIX COOKBOOK

Some of my favorite memories—and probably many of yours—are those of gathering around the table for a dinner with family and friends. But dinners like these are becoming more of a special event than a facet of daily life. Want to make them a more common event around your house? Tempt your friends and family to the table with irresistible home-baked desserts.

This doesn't have to mean spending hours in the kitchen whipping something up from scratch or doubling your grocery bill buying gourmet ingredients. Prepared cake mixes allow you to create a home-baked treat your family will love. It's easy on your wallet, and it takes almost no time at all. The trick is knowing what to do with a cake mix. This book offers recipes, tips, tricks, combinations, and preparations that will help you transform the humble box in your pantry into a favorite family dessert. Enjoy them. Have fun baking and savor the time you spend enjoying family dinners with those you love.

Cheers!

*Sarah Sawyer*

# Welcome to the EVERYTHING® Series!

These handy, accessible books give you all you need to tackle a difficult project, gain a new hobby, comprehend a fascinating topic, prepare for an exam, or even brush up on something you learned back in school but have since forgotten.

You can choose to read an Everything® book from cover to cover or just pick out the information you want from our four useful boxes: e-questions, e-facts, e-alerts, and e-ssentials.

We give you everything you need to know on the subject, but throw in a lot of fun stuff along the way, too.

We now have more than 400 Everything® books in print, spanning such wide-ranging categories as weddings, pregnancy, cooking, music instruction, foreign language, crafts, pets, New Age, and so much more. When you're done reading them all, you can finally say you know Everything®!

**QUESTION**

Answers to common questions

**FACT**

Important snippets of information

**ALERT**

Urgent warnings

**ESSENTIAL**

Quick handy tips

PUBLISHER Karen Cooper

DIRECTOR OF ACQUISITIONS AND INNOVATION Paula Munier

MANAGING EDITOR, EVERYTHING® SERIES Lisa Laing

COPY CHIEF Casey Ebert

ACQUISITIONS EDITOR Katrina Schroeder

ASSISTANT DEVELOPMENT EDITOR Elizabeth Kassab

EDITORIAL ASSISTANT Hillary Thompson

EVERYTHING® SERIES COVER DESIGNER Erin Alexander

LAYOUT DESIGNERS Colleen Cunningham, Elisabeth Lariviere, Ashley Vierra, Denise Wallace

Visit the entire Everything® series at *www.everything.com*

# THE EVERYTHING®

# CAKE MIX COOKBOOK

Sarah K. Sawyer

▲adamsmedia

Avon, Massachusetts

*To Ginny Sawyer, whose legendary*
*baking started this ball rolling.*

An Everything® Series Book.
Everything® and everything.com® are registered trademarks of F+W Media, Inc.

Published by Adams Media, a division of F+W Media, Inc.
57 Littlefield Street, Avon, MA 02322 U.S.A.
*www.adamsmedia.com*

ISBN 10: 1-60550-657-5
ISBN 13: 978-1-60550-657-9

Printed in the United States of America.

J  I  H  G  F  E  D  C  B  A

**Library of Congress Cataloging-in-Publication Data**
is available from the publisher.

*This book is available at quantity discounts for bulk purchases.*
*For information, please call 1-800-289-0963.*

# Contents

## 7  Cooking for a Crowd . . . . . . . . . . . . . . . . . . . . 99

## 8  Cooking with Kids . . . . . . . . . . . . . . . . . . . . . 117

## 9  Cake Mix Cookies . . . . . . . . . . . . . . . . . . . . . 133

# Acknowledgments

So many people have invested time and effort into making this book a success. Thank you Grandma Ginny for your baking inspiration, and to Mom for teaching me the basics of home baking. Thanks go to Brian, Ken, and Mike for offering my first opportunity to write professionally for home bakers, and to Libby for talking me through the process of recipe creation and presentation. None of this would be happening without you.

Thanks also to Bob and Katrina for seeing me through the process of writing this manuscript. Your patience and guidance are precious and made this possible. Thank you.

# Introduction

CAKES ARE THE FOOD of celebration. People bake them for the special events in life, or just to celebrate the end of a particularly lovely meal. They can have the simple flavors you'd expect from a basic cake, or they can surprise and delight the palate with unusual additions and creative ingredients. They can be homely in appearance or elaborately decorated. They can be a flavorful showcase of the cook's artistry or a fun collaboration for the kids. The possibilities are endless, and cake mix makes them easy enough for cooks of all levels.

Baking a cake is more than ticking off an item on the big night's to-do list; it's continuing a traditional art form. It's the creation of something delicious and wholesome to share with others. Every attempt to bake a cake holds within it the possibility that it will become a favorite recipe, one to be shared with friends and family and to be anticipated whenever dear ones gather.

The first step in baking a cake is, of course, planning. This doesn't have to include huge amounts of research—that's already been done. All that's really required is calmly thinking through the details. How many people are eating? Is this event fancy or family style? Do the diners enjoying this cake have dietary restrictions or allergies you must consider? Last, and most important, what recipe, ingredient, or technique would be fun to tackle next?

With these questions answered, searching for the perfect recipe is much easier. A quick glance at this book's table of contents will point you to recipes designed for holidays and special occasions as well as for family dinners. You'll also find recipes for those with special dietary needs, or cooks ready to try new ingredients. Read interesting recipes through carefully and entirely before selecting one. It's easy to miss a step, a piece of equipment, or an ingredient by reading too quickly, so take it slow. Make a list of things you need and then gather them before you start. There's nothing worse than being halfway through a project and realizing you're missing an ingredient or tool.

The must-have list of ingredients in this book starts with one thing: cake mix. Some recipes call for a specific brand or flavor, but most allow a little wiggle room. Keep a stash of basic flavors and frostings in a cool, dry cabinet and you'll be ready to bake when the event presents itself.

Now, a quick word about this main ingredient. Some feel that baking with cake mix is "cheating" and that a cake isn't truly home-baked unless the cook spent hours in the kitchen measuring, mixing, baking, frosting, and plating the picture-perfect slice. But home is where the heart is, and home-baked is anything baked with love. Most cake mixes are nothing more than basic ingredients that are simply pre-mixed for you. Why on earth not let a trusted brand do the measuring for you? It can mean a few more minutes spent living, loving, and laughing and a few less spent measuring, sifting, and sorting. Enjoying life is so much more than the icing on the cake.

# CHAPTER 1

# All about Cake Mix

It's found in a box, in many flavors, and in a certain aisle of your local grocery store, but what else do you know about cake mix? Unless you remember its debut in the late 1920s, you probably consider boxed cake mix a staple that always was and always will be—but, of course, there's more to it than that. Boxed cake mix has a cultural and culinary history that's worth knowing. Happily, this chapter is here to spill the details.

# History of Cake Baking and Innovation

Cakes were born almost the same time humans learned to make flour. Today folks around the world bake and enjoy cakes or cake-like treats, but cake was not originally developed as a dessert. The Greeks did develop cheese-cake at a very early date, and there are some records of fruitcake-like breads being baked in early Rome. In addition, ancient sweetened biscuit-style cakes have been found in Egyptian and other archeological digs. Neverthe-less, today it is generally acknowledged that the development of cake as we know it originated on the British Isles.

Most historians agree that the first records of cake were found in medi-eval England—but this was not cake as it is today. Early cakes were prob-ably nothing more than sweetened breads; in fact, for centuries the terms *cake* and *bread* were all but interchangeable. Try to imagine an early cake. Think oat bread or biscuit. They were certainly smaller in size than cakes are today, and weren't topped with a glaze, icing, or frosting.

As early as the fourteenth century, the poet Chaucer mentioned cakes made of flour, butter, eggs, cream, currants, and spices. In the seventeenth century, English writers began to describe cakes and methods for baking them. They began to sound much more like the confections we encounter today. While some cakes were still formed by hand, some were baked in tin or wooden hoops much like springform pans we use today. However, bak-ing at that time involved using a fireplace oven rather than the controllable electric and gas ovens we use today.

The first cakes were baked with no leavening at all or with yeast, but that changed in the middle of the nineteenth century. Alfred Bird's innovative baking powder made it possible to have greater leavening than ever before. This was the beginning of the spongy cake texture we enjoy today.

Around this time, the tradition of taking tea and cake in the afternoon began. Royalty started gathering for tea and small bits of layer cake with jam fillings around five o'clock in the afternoon. This was when the layer cake came into fashion.

Trends in baking came and went much as they do today. Some favorite recipes became classics and other recipes fell from favor. Flavors and fash-ions changed, but the process of baking remained mainly the same. Cake baking still required weights, measures, and elbow grease. It would be years before that changed.

# Boxed Cake Mix

Boxed cake mix was introduced in the late 1920s and early 1930s, but it was not well received at first. Cake mix languished on the shelves for twenty years before it really took off. After World War II, sales of store-bought baked goods rose, and sales of flour sank fast. Flour companies needed to find a way to encourage people to bake more to keep demand for their product high. Their answer? Make home baking faster and easier. Sell more flour in the form of cake mix.

What started as a simple marketing ploy sparked a new age of cake baking. Slowly but surely, home bakers began to see the baking of the cake itself as a simple first step. The icing, decoration, and serving of the cake became an art form. With the basic foundation of the cake perfected by flour companies, home bakers followed a few simple steps and were free to get creative with fillings, frostings, alternative preparations, and other creative treatments.

**ESSENTIAL**

All cake mixes used to include dried egg, but a consumer psychologist named Ernest Dichter found that women were afraid that baking with mixes threatened the value of their job—homemaking. Dichter recommended that companies replace the dried egg with an instruction to add fresh eggs. This seemed to make bakers feel more involved and more comfortable with the idea of baking from a mix.

Many studies regarding the use of cake mix were conducted in home economics classes all over the country. One study at Michigan State University found that the average cook saved thirteen minutes and two seconds by using cake mix.

But baking with cake mix will likely save you money in addition to time. Of course, this depends on the specific ingredients in the recipe and the cost of each ingredient.

In the end, the biggest saving that baking from a mix will bring you is the saving of mental energy. The average American cook leads a busy life filled with meeting the demands of work and family life. How many times have you heard someone say, "Oh, it takes more time to explain this than it would to do it myself?" You may have even said it yourself! This statement reflects the effort to weigh the cost of the mental energy it takes to explain a task against the physical energy and time it takes to get the job done. Often, the option that requires less mental energy wins. It's the same reason people bake with cake mix.

## The Science of Cake Mix

Have you ever wondered what's in the box? Not too surprisingly, cake mix ingredients include many of the things you'd use to bake a cake from scratch. Most cakes are composed of a base grain (flour), a sweetener (sugar), a binder (eggs), and a fat for moistness (butter). In fact, classic pound cake requires nothing more than these basic ingredients: one pound each of flour, sugar, eggs, and butter. The trick when it comes to baking is not to upset this balance of ingredients too much.

Alterations can be made, but they still must allow the basic ingredients to do their magic and produce a basic cake. If a baker wants to create something just a little richer than a basic cake, she might add extra fats. If someone else wants a denser cake, he might opt for a batter with less egg. Bakers who want a more bread-like product might add a bit more flour. There's a variation for almost every taste.

The problem here is probably pretty clear. When baking from scratch, the baker must first see that the basic chemical balance is in order. If she wants to change the cake she produces, she must find a way to do so without upsetting this balance. Again, this assumes the balance is right to begin with.

As the saying goes, "You have to know the rules before you can break them." Today's bakers are lucky. Cake mix companies learned the rules inside and out. Unless home bakers upset the cake's chemical balance in a very extreme way, they're all but guaranteed a successful cake.

## Baking Equipment

You need more than just a cake mix and the additional ingredients listed on the box to make a flawless cake. Turning out a delicious and beautiful cake takes some basic equipment. If you're sure you'll be baking, go ahead and buy the highest quality equipment you can afford. If you're relatively new to baking, you don't have to spend a lot of money on equipment. Big box and discount stores sell equipment at low prices. Also, secondhand stores and yard sales can be great places to pick up quality bakeware for spare change.

**FACT**

In *Dewey: The Small-Town Library Cat Who Touched the World,* author Vicki Myron describes a library with a collection of cake pans that library patrons could check out. This is highly unusual, but it's a great idea. Perhaps your local library would like to gather pieces and start a collection. Another option might be to loan and borrow equipment among friends who are bakers.

## Cake Pans

For even baking, a thin aluminum, stainless steel, or tin cake pan is best. These metals reflect heat and allow batter to bake evenly. Thicker, darker metals, nonstick metals, and glass pans can absorb heat and cause outer edges of your confection to overcook quickly. For best results when using a pan like this, set the oven 25 degrees lower than the temperature listed in the recipe. It's possible to bake a beautiful cake using almost any pan—the trick is to understand the personality and function of your particular equipment. Manufacturer's instructions and websites often include helpful information.

Wonder what size pan to use? Refer to pan size and shape instructions detailed on the cake mix packaging. The manufacturers pay close attention to batch volume and loft and will steer you in the right direction every time. The only exception to this rule is if you're trying to achieve an unusual shape. Then refer to recipe instructions or instructions on the pan itself.

## Cookie Sheets

Cookie sheets are often made from stainless steel, tin, or nonstick metals. They are flat. Jellyroll pans are similar but have a one-inch lip around the outer edges. Many people use them interchangeably, but the lip around the edge of the jellyroll pan can keep cookies from baking evenly.

Cookie bakers will need more than one cookie sheet. Having two will usually work; having three is a luxury.

### Measuring Tools

Because many basic ingredients are already measured out in the mix, there is usually little measuring when you bake with a cake mix. But because balancing the grains, sweetener, fats, and binders is so important, it's crucial to measure all additional ingredients exactly. All it takes is the proper equipment and a little attention to detail.

### Measuring Dry Ingredients

Making sure you have exact measurements of dry ingredients requires measuring cups and measuring spoons. Measuring cups for dry ingredients often come in a set of differently sized, clearly labeled cups. Simply fill the cup or spoon marked to hold the correct amount and level it off with a table knife or spatula. The only exception to this rule is if a recipe calls for "tightly packed" ingredients, in which case you press ingredients into the cup with a spoon or other rounded object to pack as much into the cup as possible. Brown sugar usually needs to be packed into the measuring cup.

### Wet Ingredients

Measuring cups for wet ingredients are usually glass or plastic and are printed with levels for various measurements. Because liquids shift easily, exact measurements can be difficult to read. In order to get the best possible reading, fill the cup and then set it on a level surface. Adjust your stance so that you are at eye level with the measuring line. This assures that you're not adding too much or two little due to a slant, tilt, or another shift of the level line. Newer liquid measuring cups are often designed so that you can get a correct reading from above, eliminating the need to bend over.

### About Fluid Ounces

Fluid ounces are a popular notation of measurement for wet ingredients. When this amount is listed, it is generally because the ingredient is a store-bought item with a measurement marked on the package. The marking generally exists to let you know what size package to buy in order to fill the recipe's requirement. For example, in an ingredient list, the amount of milk you need will be listed in cups, but evaporated milk will be listed in ounces. This is because you'll probably buy a gallon of milk and only use part of it for your cake, but you'll buy the exact amount of evaporated milk and use all of it to bake your cake.

You can also measure out ounces. A general rule of thumb is that 1 tablespoon is equal to ½ fluid ounce, 1 cup of liquid is equal to 8 ounces, 2 cups is equal to 16 ounces, and so on.

### Measuring Butter and Shortening

Butter and shortening are often sold in sticks. Simply slice off the amount called for according to the measurement line given on the package. If you buy margarine or shortening in a tub, you can simply spoon your ingredients into a dry measuring cup. Pack ingredients in with a spoon to eliminate bubbles, holes, or other inconsistencies that could throw off your measurement. Take care to level off the top of the cup using a knife or another utensil with a sharp edge; you don't want to use too much.

## Utensils

Baking requires basic utensils: wooden spoons, flat-edged knives for measuring, a rubber scraper for transferring ingredients, and spatulas for lifting baked cookies from sheet to wire rack. Most bakers have favorite utensils that serve them well in a variety of cooking projects. These utensils are usually among the standard favorites and are easy to find in almost any discount store.

## Tools for Mixing

Mixing thoroughly is a crucial step in most cake recipes. It's a simple step, but it does require appropriate equipment.

### Mixing Bowls

A set of mixing bowls is essential for almost any cooking project. Cake batters are fairly easy to mix and do not generally leave colors or odors behind in porous bowls, so mixing bowls made of almost any material will do. Still, a stainless steel or thick glass set of mixing bowls is a fantastic investment. Neither is porous, so they're safe from cross-contamination, and you'll be able to use them for a variety of cooking projects. They are also sturdy enough to stand up to the power of an electric beater.

Multiple mixing bowls are a good idea, even for those who wash as they go. Some recipes call for you to use bowls of different sizes.

### Electric Mixers

The taste and texture of a cake rely on the beating of the batter. If you beat it too little, your batter might taste like flour or contain lumps. If you beat it too much, the resulting cake is tougher. There was a time—and it wasn't long ago—when home bakers could achieve the perfect texture with a wooden spoon and elbow grease, but the cook who does that these days is tough to find. Most home bakers use either a tabletop mixer or handheld electric beaters. For most cake batters a hand-held mixer does the job admirably. But if you do lots of baking or think you might graduate to breads and other thicker batters, a tabletop mixer is a better fit for the job.

## Cooling Racks

A cooling rack is simply a wire rack that lifts cooling baked goods off a solid surface like a table or countertop so that they can cool. It can be tempting to skip this finishing step. Don't! Baked goods that remain in hot bakeware continue to cook. Skipping this last step can mean overcooked edges and baked goods that stick to the pan.

To successfully remove a cake layer onto a wire rack, remove the pan from the oven and put it directly onto the wire rack. Allow it to cool for about ten minutes. Loosen the layer from the side of the pan by running a knife or spatula around the edges. Place a clean linen towel or thick paper towel over the top of the layer. Place the wire rack on top of the towel. Flip the rack and the pan over at once so that the rack rests on the counter and the cake pan is upside down on top of the rack. This supports the cake while you flip it. Gently remove the pan. Once the cake is resting on the rack and free of the pan, let each cake layer cool completely before continuing with the recipe instructions. The process is tricky, but it can result in a perfect, tender layer of cake if it is approached with patience and care.

### Three First Steps

In order to have a perfect cake every time, you need to follow three easy steps.

### Read Carefully

It cannot be stressed enough that the first step in baking any cake is to read the directions thoroughly. If you are unprepared for or uncertain of any particular step, it's best to straighten it out before starting.

**ESSENTIAL**

Nonstick pans do not usually need to be treated, but they do occasionally require that you adjust cooking time or temperature to accommodate their thicker walls or treated metals. Thoroughly read the manufacturer's instructions that come with the pan or check the manufacturer's website for hints and tips specific to your particular bakeware.

### Always Preheat

Most recipes begin with preheating the oven. It is important that cake batter is exposed to an even baking temperature throughout its baking time. If the batter must sit in the oven while it heats up, it is likely the cake won't bake evenly and increases risk of burning. To prevent this, check the temperature with an oven thermometer before placing the batter in the oven. It's the surest way to protect your cake.

### Cake Pan Preparation

Many recipes will instruct you to prepare the cake pan a certain way before you add the batter. In cases where there are no specific instructions, it's a good rule of thumb to grease and flour the pan. This is easily done. Simply put a small amount of shortening or butter on wax paper and use it to evenly grease the inside of the pan. Dust the inside of the pan with a small amount of flour. Shake the pan and tap it against a solid surface to make sure the flour is evenly distributed.

Cooking sprays are a quick and effective alternative to greasing and flouring the pan. Read instructions on the package to make sure a spray-on product is safe and effective for baking.

This may feel like a lot of information upfront, but it really is important to understand the basics about your ingredients and equipment before you plan your baking project. It makes following any recipe easier and a touch more foolproof.

# CHAPTER 2

# Classic Cakes

# Bettered Box Mix

*This combination of ingredients and techniques will give you
bakery-quality results from store-bought boxed mix.*

**INGREDIENTS | SERVES 12**

1 18.25-ounce box cake mix

4 eggs

⅓ cup vegetable oil

1¼ cups cold water

1 2-ounce box pudding mix in a
   complementary flavor

1 16-ounce tub prepared frosting

## Why Not Just Follow the Instructions?

Many home bakers follow the package
instructions to the letter. It's a time-tested
way to bake a very predictable cake. But
many home bakers seek a product that is a
bit more moist and a touch more flavorful.
Adding different ingredients to the basic
building blocks in the package is the secret
to getting a professional-quality cake from
a simple boxed mix.

1. Preheat oven to 350°F. Grease and flour cake pan. Set aside.

2. Combine all ingredients in a large mixing bowl. Use an electric mixer set to medium speed to blend the batter for 6 minutes. Pour batter into the cake pan.

3. Bake according to cake mix instructions. Allow cake to cool for 10–15 minutes before inverting onto a serving plate. Cool cake completely before frosting.

# Buttermilk Cake Batter

*By changing one ingredient in the cake mix, you'll get a richer, creamier batter with a crumb that's moist and irresistible. If you don't have buttermilk handy, substitute the same amount of 2% milk with a scant splash of vinegar.*

**INGREDIENTS | SERVES 12**

1 18.25-ounce box cake mix plus ingredients called for on box (except water)

Buttermilk (equal to the amount of water called for on box)

1 16-ounce tub prepared frosting

1. Preheat oven according to cake mix instructions. Grease and flour cake pan. Set aside.

2. Mix batter according to package instructions, substituting buttermilk for water. Pour batter into cake pan. Bake according to package instructions. Cool cake.

3. Frost.

# Creamy White Cake

*White cake is a favorite flavor and a frequent base for a fancy decorated cake. Vanilla gives this cake an aromatic deliciousness, and the sour creams adds a moist richness.*

**INGREDIENTS | SERVES 8**

1 18.25-ounce package white cake mix plus ingredients called for on box

1 additional egg

2 teaspoons vanilla extract

1 cup sour cream

1 16-ounce tub prepared frosting

1. Preheat oven according to cake mix instructions. Grease and flour cake pan. Set aside.

2. Mix and batter according to instructions on box, but add the extra egg and the vanilla before you add the water.

3. When a smooth, creamy batter has formed, fold in sour cream. Bake according to instructions on the box. Cool completely before frosting.

# Lemon Chiffonette Cake

*This simple take on classic lemon chiffon cake is sure to please. The combination of lemon and vanilla creates a sweet, refreshing flavor that's perfect for summer celebrations.*

**INGREDIENTS | SERVES 8**

1 18.25-ounce box white cake mix plus ingredients called for on box
1 3.9-ounce package instant vanilla pudding mix
1 3.9-ounce package instant lemon pudding mix
1 cup milk
1 16-ounce tub whipped topping
1 pint fresh blueberries, halved

1. Preheat oven according to cake mix instructions. Grease and flour 2 round layer cake pans. Set aside.

2. Mix cake mix and vanilla pudding mix together and then follow baking directions for layers. Allow layers to cool on wire racks as you mix filling.

3. Mix lemon pudding with milk until thickened. Fold in half the whipped topping. Spread half of the filling on one layer of cake and top with blueberries.

4. Add next cake layer and top with remaining lemon filling. Frost sides of cake with remaining whipped topping. Keep cool until ready to serve.

# Nutty White Cake

*If you want to make an elaborately decorated cake, a simple recipe is the perfect way to start. The two additions to the basic cake mix in this recipe will give your baking that homemade taste and moistness you're looking for without taking all day.*

**INGREDIENTS | SERVES 8**

1 18.25-ounce box white cake mix plus ingredients called for on box
1 cup almonds, very finely ground
1 additional egg

1. Preheat oven according to cake mix instructions. Grease and flour cake pan. Set aside.

2. Add almonds to dry mix and follow mixing instructions on the package, adding the extra egg with the rest of the eggs called for. Bake according to instructions.

3. Cool completely before frosting.

# Classic Chocolate Cake

*Want cake from a box that really tastes like rich, dark chocolate? Adding a little cocoa makes the flavor boom! Don't skimp here—buy the best baking cocoa you can afford.*

**INGREDIENTS | SERVES 8**

1 18.25-ounce box chocolate cake plus all ingredients called for on box (except water)

¼ cup baking cocoa

1 additional egg

1 cup milk

1 16-ounce tub prepared frosting

1. Preheat oven according to cake mix instructions. Grease and flour cake pan. Set aside.

2. Mix cake mix according to package instructions, with these changes: add cocoa to dry ingredients; add extra egg to eggs called for on the package; and substitute the 1 cup milk for water. Bake.

3. Allow to cool completely before frosting.

## Extra Richness

Adding ½ cup finely ground nuts can be a lovely complement to a simple cake. Cashews would be a rich addition to this cake. Keep in mind, however, that some people have serious allergies to nuts. You'll want to make sure that everyone at your table is informed of your secret ingredient.

# Classic Strawberry Cake

*Opt for frozen strawberries or strawberry preserves in place of the fresh strawberries to enjoy a taste of summer on cold winter nights. For variation, try raspberries or blackberries in place of the strawberries (changing the gelatin flavor to match the berries), or lemon gelatin with berries of your choice.*

**INGREDIENTS | SERVES 8**

1 18.25-ounce package white cake mix plus ingredients called for on box
4 cups strawberries, mashed
3-ounce package strawberry gelatin
1 additional egg
1 16-ounce tub thawed whipped topping

1. Preheat oven to 350°F. Generously grease cake pan. Set aside.

2. Combine mashed strawberries and gelatin in a small bowl and set aside.

3. Prepare batter according to instructions on package, adding the additional egg. Turn batter into cake pan. Spoon strawberry mixture onto the top of the cake batter.

4. Bake for 35 minutes or until a toothpick comes out clean. Allow cake to cool completely before frosting with whipped topping.

# Italian Wedding Cake

*This is a cake for the serious sweet tooth. Pineapple, coconut, almond, and cream cheese meld with sweet white cake batter to create a rich, traditional favorite. Consider adding ½ cup finely ground almonds to the batter for an extraordinarily rich cake.*

### INGREDIENTS | SERVES 8

1 18.25-ounce box white cake mix

½ cup salted butter, softened

1¼ cups buttermilk

3 eggs

1 tablespoon vanilla extract

½ teaspoon almond extract

½ cup sweetened flaked coconut, flaked

1 8-ounce can crushed pineapple, drained

2 cups chopped pecans

2 16-ounce tubs cream cheese frosting

1. Preheat oven to 350°F. Grease cake pan and set aside.

2. Combine cake mix, butter, buttermilk, eggs, vanilla extract, and almond extract in a large mixing bowl.

3. Using an electric mixer set to low speed, beat until completely smooth and combined. Fold in coconut, pineapple, and half the pecans. Pour into cake pan.

4. Bake for 35 minutes or until a toothpick comes out clean. Allow cake to cool completely before turning onto serving platter.

5. Meanwhile, mix remaining nuts and frosting. When cake is cool, frost and serve!

# Devil's Food Cake

*The decadence of devil's food cake and the sweet, rich taste and slightly chewy texture of coconut make this dessert a real treat. The whipped topping lightens things up. For a quick variation, top this cake with cherry pie filling and whipped cream instead of the whipped topping.*

**INGREDIENTS | SERVES 8**

1 18-ounce box devil's food cake mix plus ingredients called for on box
1 additional egg
2 cups sour cream
2 cups coconut
1 16-ounce tub whipped topping

1. Preheat oven to 350°F. Grease and flour two layer cake pans. Set aside.

2. Mix according to cake mix instructions, adding the extra egg with the eggs called for in the directions. Bake according to package directions for a two-layer cake.

3. As cake cools, mix sour cream, coconut, and whipped topping in a bowl. When layers are cool, use this mixture to frost as you would a two-layer cake.

# Neon Angel Cake

*Don't be afraid to get crazy now and then. Slices of star fruit may give your artistic creation that star quality you're looking for.*

**INGREDIENTS | SERVES 8**

1 18.25-ounce box angel food cake mix plus ingredients called for on box
1 3-ounce package instant gelatin in a wild, neon color/flavor
Food coloring
Whipped topping

1. Preheat oven according to cake mix instructions. Grease and flour cake pan. Set aside.

2. Mix batter according to instructions. Add gelatin to batter spoonful by spoonful until you reach desired color/flavor intensity. Bake cake according to package instructions.

3. Cool cake completely. Meanwhile, mix food coloring and whipped topping to desired color. Frost cake with whipped topping for a color-crazy surprise.

# Chocolate Bundt Cake

*The blend of real chocolate morsels and flavorful vanilla pudding are the power combination that enhances the flavor of this favorite cake.*

**INGREDIENTS | SERVES 8**

1 18.25-ounce box marble cake mix
4 eggs
½ cup oil
1 cup milk
1 3.9-ounce box instant vanilla pudding mix
½ cup chocolate chips
1 16-ounce tub prepared frosting

1. Preheat oven to 350°F. Grease and flour a 12-cup bundt pan. Set aside.

2. In a large bowl, combine cake mix, eggs, oil, and milk. Mix until a smooth batter forms.

3. Reserve 1 cup of the batter. Pour the rest into the prepared bundt pan. In a small bowl, combine the reserved cup of batter with the chocolate powder.

4. Fold chocolate chips into chocolate mixture. Spoon chocolate mixture on top of batter.

5. Cut through each spoonful of chocolate mixture a few times with a knife to create a marbled batter. Bake for 35 minutes or until a toothpick comes out clean.

6. Allow cake to cool completely before turning onto serving platter to frost.

# Lemon Cooler Cake

*Because this cake is best when flavors are allowed to combine during chilling, this is a fantastic choice to prepare ahead of time.*

1. Preheat oven according to cake mix instructions. Grease and flour two layer cake pans. Set aside.

2. Mix cake according to instructions for two-layer cake. Remove from oven and allow to cool completely. Lay cooled cake layer on a clean, flat surface. Mark the middle of the cake layer with toothpicks. With toothpicks as your guide, slice cake horizontally, using a few slow, even strokes of a serrated knife. Carefully remove top layer to a clean, flat surface. Repeat this process with the second layer to create four layers total.

3. Combine condensed milk and lemon juice. Reserve half of the mixture. Spread one-third of the remaining mixture on one layer; top with another layer and repeat. Do not spread mixture on top of fourth layer.

4. Combine remaining mixture with whipped topping to create frosting. Frost cake. Chill 24 hours before serving.

# Earth Angel Food Cake

*The chemistry of a well-baked cake is a delicate balancing game—especially with the light and airy angel food cake. However, adding an extra egg white gives you a richer texture and taste!*

**INGREDIENTS** | **SERVES 8**

1 box angel food cake mix plus ingredients called for on box

1 additional egg white

Whipped topping

Fresh fruit of choice

1. Preheat oven according to cake mix instructions. Grease and flour cake pan. Set aside.

2. Mix batter according to instructions, adding extra egg white with the rest of the eggs. Bake according to instructions.

3. Allow cake to cool completely before topping with whipped topping and fresh fruit.

# Chocolate Chip Cookie Cake

*When comfort food is the name of the game, there's nothing better than a chocolate chip cookie. This recipe captures the flavor in a light, delicious cake.*

**INGREDIENTS** | **SERVES 8**

1 18.25-ounce box yellow cake mix plus ingredients called for on box

1 additional egg

1 12-ounce package semisweet chocolate morsels

1 16-ounce tub prepared frosting

1. Preheat oven according to cake mix instructions. Grease and flour cake pan. Set aside.

2. Mix cake according to instructions, adding extra egg with the other eggs. When batter is smooth, fold in chocolate chips. Pour batter into a cake pan.

3. Bake according to instructions on the package. Cool and frost.

# Peachy Yellow Cake

*Baby food is the secret ingredient in this delicately flavored cake. Lower in fat than most cakes and light in flavor, this cake is great with a cold glass of milk.*

**INGREDIENTS | SERVES 8**

1 18.25-ounce box yellow cake mix plus ingredients called for on box (except oil)

1 additional egg

1 4-ounce jar peach baby food

1 16-ounce tub prepared frosting

### Peaches and More

Bakers have long substituted a fruit purée for oil when baking with prepared mixes. It often yields a more complex flavor and more homemade texture. You can use any purée you like, so feel free to experiment with mixes and fruits. You'll love testing the results.

1. Preheat oven to 350°F. Grease and flour cake pan. Set aside.

2. Mix batter according to instructions on the package, adding the extra egg with the other eggs and substituting the baby food for the oil.

3. Bake cake according to instructions on the box. Remove from oven and allow cake to cool completely before frosting.

# Fluffiest Cake Ever

*Recipes like this one are the darlings of cake decorators who long for a home-baked taste. Meringue powder and extra egg give this cake the same lightness and loft of a bakery cake.*

**INGREDIENTS | SERVES 8**

1 18.25-ounce box cake mix without pudding, plus ingredients called for on box

2 tablespoons meringue powder

1 extra egg

1. Preheat oven according to cake mix instructions. Grease cake pan and set aside.

2. Add meringue powder to dry ingredients and mix according to package instructions, adding the extra egg with the other eggs.

3. Beat batter for 5 minutes using an electric mixer set to medium speed. Turn batter into the pan and bake according to package instructions.

4. Allow cake to cool completely before frosting and decorating.

# Simply Better Chocolate Cake

*This recipe takes just a little extra measuring, but the results are well worth it. With cocoa and sugar for extra sweet richness, this is a great foundation recipe for all your fancy cake decoration projects.*

**INGREDIENTS** | **SERVES 8**

1 18.25-ounce box chocolate cake mix plus ingredients called for on box

2 tablespoons cornstarch

3 tablespoons cocoa

1 additional egg

½ cup sugar

1 16-ounce tub prepared frosting

1. Preheat oven according to cake mix instructions. Grease and flour cake pan. Set aside.

2. In a large mixing bowl, combine cake mix and ingredients called for on box. Add cornstarch, cocoa, extra egg, and sugar. Stir to combine. Add additional egg.

3. Beat batter for 5 minutes using an electric mixer set to medium speed. Pour batter into cake pan. Bake cake according to instructions on package.

4. Allow cake to cool completely before turning out onto serving platter. Frost.

# Vanilla Cake

*In ancient times, vanilla was known as an aphrodisiac. Today it's the smell
of someone baking with love for those close to her heart.*

**INGREDIENTS | SERVES 12**

1 18.25-ounce box white cake mix
½ cup butter, softened
½ cup sugar
4 eggs
4½ teaspoons vanilla extract
¼ teaspoon baking powder
1 cup milk
1 16-ounce tub prepared frosting

### Buying Vanilla

Vanilla can be bought in natural (bean) and processed (extract) forms. If you like very strong flavor, you might prefer vanilla extract. If, however, you prefer a more subtle taste and aroma, consider vanilla beans. If you're feeling extra festive, split the bean lengthwise, remove the tiny seeds, and incorporate them into your batter.

1. Preheat oven to 350°F. Grease and flour cake pan. Set aside.

2. Cream butter and sugar using an electric mixer set to medium speed.

3. Slowly incorporate cake mix and all remaining ingredients except frosting, beating for 4 minutes. The batter should be light and smooth. Turn batter into cake pan.

4. Bake for 30 minutes or until a toothpick comes out clean. Allow cake to cool completely before frosting.

# Mega-Moist Chocolate Cake

*The addition of extra eggs and sour cream give this cake the same spongy spring found in a cake you'd bake from scratch. You can get creative here by adding a little extra cocoa, some chocolate morsels, or almost anything else that strikes your fancy.*

**INGREDIENTS | SERVES 8**

1 18.25-ounce box chocolate cake mix
1 cup sour cream
1 cup vegetable oil
4 eggs
½ cup water
1 16-ounce tub prepared frosting

1. Preheat oven to 350°F. Grease and flour cake pan. Set aside.

2. In a large mixing bowl, combine cake mix, sour cream, oil, eggs, and water. Pour into a cake pan. Bake for 50 minutes.

3. Remove from oven and allow to cool completely before turning onto a plate. Frost when entirely cool.

# Simply Better Yellow Cake

*This recipe is great for a cake that requires you to pour your concentration into decoration. It's simple, reliable, and lovely. Substitute other cake mix flavors for variety.*

**INGREDIENTS | SERVES 8**

1 18.25-ounce box yellow cake mix plus ingredients called for on box (except water)

Whole milk in the same amount as water called for on box

1 additional egg

1 16-ounce tub prepared frosting

1. Preheat oven according to cake mix instructions. Grease and flour cake pan. Set aside.

2. Mix batter according to package instructions, substituting whole milk for water and adding the extra egg with the other eggs.

3. Using an electric mixer set to medium speed, beat batter until it is smooth and entirely lump-free. Pour batter into cake pan. Bake according to instructions.

4. Allow cake to cool completely before frosting.

# CHAPTER 3

# Birthday Cakes

# Baby's First Cake

*What better way to celebrate the close of a year of feedings, late nights, and precious parenting moments than by incorporating baby's favorite food into a cake everyone will enjoy? You can use any sweet baby food in this recipe.*

**INGREDIENTS | SERVES 12**

1 18.25-ounce box moist yellow cake mix
½ cup white sugar
1 cup vegetable oil
4 eggs
1 4-ounce jar apricot baby food
1 4-ounce jar plum baby food
1 16-ounce tub prepared frosting

## Decorating Baby's Cake

It may be tempting to paint up this cake with frosting roses or other elaborate decorations, but remember, baby is going to eat this cake—and the sugar can be just too much. Consider using less frosting or even substituting whipped cream for frosting. The cake will be yummy, and little partiers will stay happier longer.

1. Preheat oven to 375°F. Grease and flour a 10" bundt pan. Set aside.

2. Combine all ingredients except frosting in a large mixing bowl. Blend with an electric mixer on medium speed until a smooth batter forms.

3. Pour cake mixture evenly into the pan. Bake for 1 hour. Remove from oven and let cool in the pan.

4. Tip pan onto serving plate and allow gravity to let cake drop. Frost with desired frosting.

# Birthday Cake in a Cone

*Easy to eat and fun to bake, this is the perfect way to bake up a little fun on birthdays, rainy days, or any other day you choose.*

**INGREDIENTS | SERVES 36**

1 18.25-ounce box white cake mix plus ingredients called for on box

36 ice cream cones

Dark chocolate chips

36 scoops ice cream

Sprinkles

1. Preheat oven to temperature listed on the box in cupcake instructions. Prepare batter according to instructions on the package.

2. Place 2 tablespoons cake batter in each ice cream cone and top with chocolate chips.

3. Place cones on cookie sheet and bake according to instructions on cake mix package. Remove from oven and allow to cool completely.

4. Top each cone/cake with a scoop of ice cream. Allow guests to decorate their cones with sprinkles.

# PB&J Cupcakes

*PB&J is a winning flavor combination with the young and the young at heart. The combination
of rich protein and sweet fruity preserves makes a perfect, wholesome treat.
These cupcakes are a surprising way to enjoy an old favorite.*

**INGREDIENTS | SERVES 24**

1 18.25-ounce package yellow cake mix
plus ingredients called for on box
(except oil)

1 cup creamy peanut butter

½ cup jelly

24 paper baking cups

1 16-ounce tub prepared frosting

1. Preheat oven to 350°F. Line muffin pan with 24 paper baking cups. Set aside.

2. Beat cake mix and peanut butter using an electric mixer on medium speed until crumbs form. Then continue according to the instructions on the cake mix package, omitting oil.

3. Fill each muffin cup halfway. You should have batter remaining when finished. Add 1 teaspoon jelly to each cup.

4. Cover jelly with batter so that the paper cup is ¾ full and the jelly is covered entirely. Bake cupcakes for 24 minutes, or until a toothpick comes out clean.

5. Remove pan to a wire rack and allow cupcakes to cool for 15 minutes. Remove cupcakes from pan and allow to cool completely before frosting.

# Birthday Cake with Sprinkles

*Colorful and festive sprinkles are a sure sign that a celebration is afoot. Dress up a weeknight dinner or create a birthday masterpiece with this playful recipe.*

**INGREDIENTS  |  SERVES 12**

1 18.25-ounce box white cake mix with pudding
¾ cup water
½ cup sour cream
2 eggs
1 16-ounce tub prepared frosting
Sprinkles

1. Preheat oven to 350°F. Grease and flour cake pan. Set aside.

2. Mix all ingredients together to form a smooth batter. Turn batter into pan and bake 25 minutes.

3. Allow cake to cool completely before frosting. Frost cake evenly and top with cheerful sprinkles.

## Simple Pleasures

We are often tempted to pull out the stops to create a complicated character cake or spend large amounts of money at a local bakery in order to delight a birthday celebrant—but there's something delightful about a home-baked cake. Top it with brightly colored sprinkles and you have a cake that's a feast for the eyes and the taste buds.

# Princess Pink Strawberry Cake

*There's just something about pink—the sweet strawberry colors and creamy add-ins
make for a Southern-style cake fit for a party of extra-girly proportions.*

**INGREDIENTS | SERVES 12**

1 18.25-ounce box white cake mix

1 cup mayonnaise

2 tablespoons flour

1 3-ounce package strawberry gelatin

4 eggs

½ cup cold water

½ 10-ounce package frozen
strawberries, thawed

## Strawberry Frosting

Reserve the liquid from the package of frozen strawberries for this frosting. Combine
2 tablespoons melted butter, 3 tablespoons strawberry liquid, and 1 cup confectioners' sugar to make a naturally pink
frosting for this strawberry cake.

1. Preheat oven to 350°F. Grease and flour cake pan. Set
   aside.

2. Combine cake mix, mayonnaise, flour, gelatin, and
   eggs. Mix well to form a smooth batter. Fold in water
   and strawberries.

3. Turn batter into pan. Bake for 45 minutes. Allow cake
   to cool completely before frosting.

# Flower Pot Trifle

*You can personalize this cake by adding plastic fairies or creepy bugs. The magic ingredient here is your imagination. Serve it in the garden for a playful presentation.*

**INGREDIENTS | SERVES 12**

1 large 18-ounce package chocolate sandwich cookies with crème filling

¼ cup butter, softened

1 8-ounce package cream cheese

¾ cup confectioners' sugar

2 3.9-ounce packages instant vanilla pudding mix

2¾ cups cold milk

1 12-ounce tub nondairy whipped topping

1 clean, 8" porcelain or terra cotta flower pot

Gummy worms

Clean plastic flowers or grasses

1. Place cookies in a plastic bag or blender and crush completely. Set aside.

2. In a large bowl, mix butter, cream cheese, and confectioners' sugar.

3. In a separate bowl, mix together the vanilla pudding and milk. Add to butter mixture, and then add nondairy whipped topping.

4. Pour batter and crushed cookies into the flower pot in alternating layers, starting and ending with a cookie layer. Refrigerate for 12 hours to set.

5. Garnish with gummy worms and plastic flowers.

# Belle of the Ball Fashion Doll Cake

*Whether made simply or with elaborate decoration, the doll cake is an enduring favorite. Perfect for a birthday party or for other girly gatherings.*

**INGREDIENTS | SERVES 12**

1 18.25-ounce box white cake mix plus ingredients called for on box

1 16-ounce tub prepared frosting

Clean 12" fashion doll

### Simple Piping

To create simple designs, fill a sandwich bag with icing, snip one bottom corner, and squeeze the bag to create dots, lines, and other details. Start with lines or cursive writing, and work up to dots and more complicated patterns. It might take a little practice, but the end result is worth it!

1. Preheat oven to 350°F. Grease and flour a 2-quart ovenproof Pyrex bowl.

2. Mix cake batter according to package directions and pour into the bowl. Bake for 60 minutes or until a toothpick comes out clean.

3. Remove cake from oven and allow to cool in the bowl for 15 minutes. Invert the bowl over a serving plate. Allow gravity to pull the cake out of the bowl.

4. Allow cake to set for 3½ hours before icing. Insert a clean fashion doll feet first into the cake so that the cake becomes the doll's skirt.

5. Frost the cake and a bodice onto the doll so that the icing creates a dress for the doll.

# All-American Burger Cake

*Sliders (mini burgers) are a trendy appetizer in many restaurants. To mimic this trend, create cupcake-sized versions of this cake.*

**INGREDIENTS | SERVES 12**

1 18.25-ounce box white cake mix plus ingredients called for on box

1 18.25-ounce brownie mix plus ingredients called for on box

1 12-ounce can ready-to-spread vanilla frosting

1 12-ounce can ready-to-spread chocolate frosting

Red food coloring

Yellow food coloring

¼ cup granulated sugar

1. Preheat oven to 350°F. Generously grease two 8" layer pans.

2. Prepare and bake white cake mix according to package directions. Remove from oven and let cool for 20 minutes. Remove cakes from pans to wire racks and allow to cool completely.

3. While cake layers cool, prepare brownies according to package directions and bake in an 8" layer pan. Remove from oven and allow to cool for 15 minutes in the pan. Invert pan and allow layer to cool on a wire rack.

4. Reserve 1 cup vanilla frosting. Mix remaining vanilla frosting and all of chocolate frosting together with a drop each of red and yellow food colorings to create the color of a bun.

5. Place one cake layer on serving plate; cut off the top if it is too rounded to sit flat. Frost with half of the bun-colored frosting. Top with brownie layer.

6. In separate bowls, mix some vanilla frosting with yellow coloring for mustard and red for ketchup. Top brownie with frosting.

7. Add top layer of cake and frost with remaining bun-colored frosting.

# Yellow Pop Cake

*This recipe has that certain "mad scientist" feel to it, and it goes great with pizza.*

**INGREDIENTS | SERVES 12**

1 18.25-ounce box lemon cake mix

½ cup oil

1 3.9-ounce box pineapple instant pudding mix

1 8-ounce can Mountain Dew

6 eggs, divided use

½ cup butter

½ cup sugar

1 cup crushed pineapple, drained.

1. Preheat oven to 350°F. Grease and flour two 9" cake layer pans. Set aside.

2. Combine cake mix, oil, pudding mix, Mountain Dew, and 4 of the eggs in a large mixing bowl. Turn batter into pans. Bake for 25 minutes.

3. Meanwhile, combine remaining 2 eggs, butter, sugar, and crushed pineapple in a small saucepan and warm over low heat until thickened.

4. Remove cake from oven and allow to cool for 10 minutes in the pan before removing to a wire rack. Frost while still warm.

# Birthday Cake Ice Cream

*This recipe lets you honor the tradition of having a birthday cake while skipping the baking altogether. It's a particularly big hit on hot summer birthdays.*

**INGREDIENTS | SERVES 5**

⅔ cup granulated sugar

1 cup whole milk, chilled

2 cups heavy cream, chilled

1 teaspoon vanilla extract

⅔ cup confetti cake mix

Ice cream maker

1. Dissolve sugar into milk by whisking briskly. Add heavy cream and vanilla. Mix well. Sift in cake mix to avoid lumps.

2. Add mixture to an ice cream maker and follow instructions given for the appliance.

### Think Outside the Box

Birthday cake doesn't always have to be a cake, nor does it require candles or frosting or any other traditional elements. The truly important part of the celebration is that the birthday celebrant feels special. If an ice cream cake will make her smile, then go that route.

# Peanut Butter Cup Cake

*Themed cakes like this one are a special treat with a personalized touch.*
*Peanut butter candies make a tasty addition to this recipe.*

**INGREDIENTS | SERVES 24**

1 18.25-ounce box yellow cake and ingredients called for on package instructions.
¼ cup water
10 peanut butter cups, quartered
1 12-ounce tub cream cheese frosting
Whole peanut butter cups for garnish

1. Preheat oven to 350°F. Grease and flour cake pan. Set aside.

2. Combine cake mix and all ingredients called for on the box as instructed, and add an extra ¼ cup of water.

3. Fold in the candy chunks. Turn batter into prepared cake pan and bake for 45 minutes.

4. Remove cake from heat and allow to cool 15 minutes before turning out onto serving platter.

5. Frost cake and garnish with whole peanut butter cups. Consider using the candies as a base for birthday candles.

# Swirl Cake

*Can't decide between chocolate cake and confetti cake? Choose two different flavors of cake mix for this recipe. Almost anything goes. Experiment with flavors, but remember that sometimes less is more.*

**INGREDIENTS | SERVES 15**

2 18.25-ounce boxes cake mix plus ingredients called for on boxes
2 12-ounce tubs prepared frosting

1. Preheat oven to 350°F. Grease and flour an 18" × 13" cake pan. Set aside. Mix the first box of cake mix according to instructions on the box. In a separate bowl, mix the second box of cake mix.

2. Spoon a strip of the first cake batter into pan. Then spoon in a strip of the second batter. Alternate strips until the pan is filled.

3. Using a knife, cut through the batter so that the two cake batters mix and marble. Bake according to instructions on the package.

4. Allow cake to cool completely before frosting.

# Lemony Birthday Cake

*This light and fruity cake—made with real juice—is perfect for a luncheon or for a springtime birthday. Its refreshing and lighter taste make it an instant favorite.*

**INGREDIENTS | SERVES 12**

1 18.25-ounce box lemon cake mix
½ cup sugar
4 eggs
1 cup orange juice
½ cup shortening
1 cup confectioners' sugar
Juice from 1 lemon

## Shopping for Lemons

Lemons that are best for juicing feel heavier than expected. Smooth-skinned lemons tend to be easier to juice and will give a better yield, which means more flavor for your cake. Consider organic lemons. They may not look as pretty as the huge, waxed, conventional ones, but their taste is often purer.

1. Preheat oven to 350°F. Grease a 12-cup bundt pan and set aside.

2. Mix first five ingredients in a large bowl with an electric mixer set to medium speed until a smooth batter forms. Turn batter into the pan.

3. Bake for 45 minutes or until a toothpick comes out clean. Remove from oven and allow to cool for 15 minutes before inverting the pan over a serving plate.

4. Using a fork, thoroughly mix confectioners' sugar and lemon juice. Drizzle over warm cake.

# Cookies and Cream Birthday Cake

*There's something so comforting about the taste (and crunch) of a classic sandwich cookie. Serve this cake with ice cold milk for a wholesome treat.*

**INGREDIENTS** | **SERVES 8**

1 18.25-ounce box devil's food chocolate cake mix plus ingredients called for on box

4 squares semisweet baking chocolate

¼ cup butter

1 8-ounce package softened cream cheese

½ cup granulated sugar

2 cups nondairy whipped topping

12 chocolate sandwich cookies, crushed

Whole sandwich cookies for garnish

## Complementing Cookies

Nothing goes better with a cookie than cold milk. But if milk's not your cup of tea—well, consider tea. (Coffee or punch also work.) The cake is often the focus of the birthday, but beverages are important too, especially for young guests. Soft drinks are often too sweet to complement cakes, but milk and lemonade do nicely.

1. Preheat oven to 350°F. Grease and flour two layer cake pans. Set aside.

2. Prepare and bake cake according to instructions on box for a two-layer cake.

3. Remove baked cakes from oven and allow to cool for 5 minutes before removing to wire racks to cool completely.

4. Meanwhile, make chocolate glaze by melting chocolate and butter in the microwave. Melt for 1 minute on medium high. Remove from microwave. Stir. Continue to microwave in 10-second intervals until the mixture is smooth and creamy. Cool for 5 minutes.

5. In a large bowl, mix cream cheese and sugar until well blended. Fold in whipped topping and crushed sandwich cookies.

6. Spread cream cheese filling between the two layers of cake. Cover top layer of cake with the chocolate glaze.

7. Tile the top of the cake with round halves of sandwich cookies (twist to separate) for an elegant effect.

# Tropical Birthday Cake

*This rich, sweet cake is perfect for a sultry summer birthday.*
*You'll need to keep it refrigerated, so serve it close to home.*

### INGREDIENTS | SERVES 12

1 18.25-ounce package white cake mix plus ingredients called for on box

1 14-ounce can cream of coconut

1 14-ounce can sweetened condensed milk

¾ cup pineapple juice

1 16-ounce tub whipped topping

## Decorating the Tropical Birthday Cake

This moist, sweet treat may not have the look you expect for a birthday cake, but it's nonetheless great for a grown-up get-together. Garnish with coconut, pineapple rings, colored sugar, or even edible flowers like pansies to create a special feel.

1. Preheat oven to 350°F. Grease and flour 9" × 13" cake pan. Set aside.

2. Mix batter according to instructions on the package. Turn batter into cake pan; bake according to instructions. Remove from oven.

3. While the cake is still hot, poke holes in it using a long-pronged fork.

4. Combine cream of coconut, condensed milk, and pineapple juice. Mix well. Pour over the warm cake so that it fills holes poked in the cake. Let cake cool completely.

5. Frost cake with whipped topping. Refrigerate until ready to serve.

# Éclair Birthday Cake

*There's a creamy richness to this cake that recalls an indulgent custard-filled éclair. Serve with hot coffee for a lovely treat.*

### INGREDIENTS | SERVES 15

- 1 18.25-ounce box fudge chocolate cake mix, plus ingredients called for on box
- 4 cups ricotta cheese
- 1 cup sugar
- 4 eggs
- 1 teaspoon vanilla
- 1 3.9-ounce box instant chocolate pudding mix
- 1 cup milk
- 1 8-ounce tub nondairy whipped topping

1. Preheat oven to 350°F. Grease and flour 9" × 13" cake pan. Set aside.

2. Prepare cake batter according to instructions on the package and pour into pan.

3. In a mixing bowl, combine cheese, sugar, eggs, and vanilla. Blend completely and layer over cake batter. Bake according to cake mix instructions.

4. Remove cake from oven and allow to cool completely.

5. While cake cools, mix pudding, milk, and whipped topping. Spread over cake. Refrigerate until ready to serve.

# Pizza Cake

*Bake smaller cakes using mini quiche pans or ramekins. Allow guests to decorate their own pizzas.*

**INGREDIENTS | SERVES 12**

1 18.25-ounce box yellow cake mix plus ingredients called for on box

1 tub 12-ounce prepared vanilla frosting

Red food coloring

1 tub 12-ounce prepared frosting (caramel color to be "crust")

Sliced fruit for toppings

Shredded coconut for "cheese"

1. Preheat oven according to cake mix instructions. Grease and flour a round cake pan. Set aside.

2. Prepare and bake cake according to package instructions. Allow cake to cool completely before inverting onto serving plate to decorate.

3. Add red food coloring drop by drop to vanilla frosting to create "sauce." Frost the top of the cake with red frosting and the sides with caramel-colored frosting.

4. Place sliced fruit on cake to resemble pizza toppings and sprinkle lightly with coconut to resemble cheese.

# Crust for Ice Cream Pie

*These crusts are a perfect complement to cake batter ice cream. Make two batches of ice cream for a pie your guests will flip over!*

**INGREDIENTS | MAKES 2 PIE CRUSTS**

1 18.25-ounce package chocolate cake mix

1 16-ounce tub prepared chocolate frosting

¾ cup water

1 cup semi sweet chocolate chips

1. Preheat oven to 350°F. Grease pie pans generously with shortening.

2. In a large mixing bowl, combine cake mix, frosting, and water. Mix well. Pat half the mixture into one pie pan and repeat for the second pan.

3. Bake for 20–24 minutes or until the crusts are slightly plumped. Cool in pans.

### Creating an Ice Cream Pie

You'll use 4 cups (1 quart) of ice cream for each pie. Allow the ice cream to soften before spooning it into the pie crust. Shape it using a flat spoon. Top with ice cream toppings, sprinkles, nuts, or anything else you fancy. Freeze pie until firm. Remove from freezer 20 minutes before serving. This pie is perfect for a birthday or festive occasion.

# Boston Crème Cake

*Creamy custard-like filling and extra sweet chocolate topping recall the flavor of Boston cream pie. This easy-to-bake cake is sure to impress.*

## INGREDIENTS | SERVES 12

- 1 18.25-ounce box vanilla cake mix plus ingredients called for on box
- 1 3.9-ounce package instant French vanilla pudding mix plus ingredients for making pie filling
- 1 12-ounce package semisweet chocolate morsels
- ½ cup heavy whipping cream

1. Preheat oven according to cake mix instructions. Grease and flour two layer cake pans. Set aside.

2. Prepare cake batter and bake according to package instructions for a two-layer cake. Remove from oven and allow to cool completely.

3. As cake cools, prepare pudding mix according to directions for pie filling found on pudding package.

4. Lay cooled cake layers on a clean, flat surface. Mark the middle of the cake layer with toothpicks. With toothpicks as your guide, slice layer horizontally, using a few slow, even strokes of a serrated knife. Carefully remove top layer to a clean, flat surface. Repeat this process with the second layer to create four layers total. Spread pie filling evenly between the layers.

5. In a microwave-safe bowl, combine chocolate morsels and heavy cream. Microwave for 1 minute. Remove from microwave and stir until smooth.

6. Pour chocolate over cake, spreading evenly with rubber spatula. Allow cake to cool for 2 hours in the refrigerator before serving.

# Black Forest Birthday Cake

*Cherries and chocolate are always a winning pair. This sweet, rich, sophisticated cake is a special treat for a chocolate lover's birthday.*

**INGREDIENTS | SERVES 12**

1 18.25-ounce package chocolate cake mix

1 21-ounce can cherry pie filling

2 eggs

⅓ cup vegetable oil

1 teaspoon almond extract

1 cup granulated sugar

5 tablespoons butter

⅓ cup milk

1 cup chocolate chips

1. Preheat oven to 350°F. Grease and flour cake pan. Set aside.

2. In a large bowl, combine cake mix, pie filling, eggs, oil, and almond extract. Mix to form a smooth batter. Bake for 30 minutes.

3. Meanwhile, combine remaining ingredients in a saucepan, bringing gently to a boil. Stir until smooth and use to frost warm cake.

# Cherry Cordial Birthday Cake

*This cake has it all. Rich cake, creamy pudding, cherry flavor, chocolate morsels, and gooey candies on top. This sweet, sensual treat wins your sweet tooth right over and makes a lovely presentation.*

**INGREDIENTS | SERVES 12**

1 18.25-ounce box chocolate cake mix

1 3.9-ounce package instant chocolate pudding mix

4 eggs

1¼ cups water

½ cup vegetable oil

1 tablespoon cherry extract or flavor

1 cup chocolate morsels

1 tub prepared chocolate frosting

Cherry cordial candies to garnish

1. Preheat oven to 350°F. Grease and flour cake pan. Set aside.

2. In a large mixing bowl, combine cake mix, pudding mix, eggs, water, oil, and extract. Blend using an electric mixer set to low speed for 2 minutes.

3. Pour batter into a cake pan. Sprinkle chocolate morsels evenly on top of wet cake batter. Bake for 55 minutes. Let cake cool completely before frosting and decorating with candies.

# CHAPTER 4

# Family Favorites

# Chess Cake

*There are times when you want a dessert with an artful presentation—and times when you want a wholesome sweet to finish a weekday meal. Chess cake is a perfect everyday treat, and leftovers will keep well enough to enjoy another night.*

**INGREDIENTS | SERVES 12**

1 18.25-ounce box yellow cake mix
4 eggs, divided
1 cup butter, melted, divided
1 8-ounce package cream cheese
4 cups confectioners' sugar

1. Preheat oven to 350°F. Grease and flour a 9" × 13" cake pan. Set aside.

2. Mix cake mix, 2 of the eggs, and ½ cup of the melted butter in a large bowl. Turn batter into pan.

3. Mix cream cheese with the remaining ½ cup butter and two eggs in a separate bowl. Fold confectioners' sugar into cream cheese mixture.

4. Layer cream cheese mixture over batter in pan. Bake for 1 hour. Cool in the pan.


# Chess Cake Squares

*This recipe makes a slightly more solid "bar" than the cake recipe. Easy to cut and serve, it's a great choice for potlucks and other events as it travels very well.*

**INGREDIENTS | SERVES 12**

1 18.25-ounce box yellow or butter cake mix
½ cup butter
4 eggs, divided use
½ cup white sugar
1 8-ounce package cream cheese, softened

1. Preheat oven to 350°F. Grease and flour a 9" × 13" pan. Set aside.

2. In a large bowl, mix cake mix, butter, and 1 egg until a shortbread-like mixture forms. Pat mixture into the bottom of the pan.

3. In a separate bowl, combine sugar, remaining eggs, and softened cream cheese. Layer on top of crust. Bake for 40 minutes or until slightly browned.

4. Allow to cool in the pan before scoring into bars.

# Butter Cake

*This Southern favorite offers a mild taste and creamy texture that's sure to be the belle of any dinner you attend. Every family has a recipe for butter cake—but yours is the easiest.*

**INGREDIENTS | SERVES 12**

1 18.25-ounce package yellow cake mix
½ cup butter
3 eggs, divided
1 8-ounce package cream cheese
1 1-pound box confectioners' sugar
1 teaspoon vanilla

1. Preheat oven to 350°F.

2. Combine cake mix, butter, and 1 egg until a shortbread-like batter forms. Pat this mixture into an ungreased 9" × 13" pan.

3. Using a wooden spoon, combine cream cheese, remaining 2 eggs, confectioners' sugar, and vanilla.

4. Layer cream cheese mixture over cake mixture, covering cake batter completely. Bake for 35 minutes.

# Peachy Skillet Bake

*Peaches are particularly delicate fruits. Overripe peaches can become grainy—definitely not a texture you want for your baked goods. Always select ripe peaches with a firm texture for the sweetness you want for this and other desserts.*

**INGREDIENTS | SERVES 12**

1 15-ounce can sliced peaches in syrup
1 18.25-ounce box white cake mix
½ cup butter

1. Preheat oven to 350°F.

2. Pour peaches and juice into a hot oven-safe 12" skillet. Cover the peaches with dry cake mix and dot with pats of butter. Cover and bake for 40 minutes.

# Harvest Fruit Bake

*Autumn is a time to enjoy the harvest—and this recipe is a wonderful excuse to do so. Canned fruits make it easy. Top with whipped cream for an irresistible autumn treat.*

**INGREDIENTS | SERVES 12**

1 21-ounce can peach pie filling
1 16-ounce can whole cranberry sauce
½ teaspoon ground cinnamon
¼ teaspoon ground nutmeg
1 18.25-ounce box yellow cake mix
1 cup cold butter

1. Preheat oven to 350°F.

2. Mix peach pie filling and cranberry sauce and turn into an ungreased 9" × 13" pan.

3. In a separate bowl, add spices to dry cake mix and cut in butter. Sprinkle over fruit mixture. Bake for 45 minutes. Allow to cool 15 minutes before serving.

# Quickest Brownies

*Nothing beats homemade brownies. Whip up this treat any night of the week for a sweet end to a great meal.*

**INGREDIENTS | SERVES 12**

1 18.25-ounce box chocolate cake mix
½ cup butter, melted
2 eggs, divided
½ box confectioners' sugar
1 8-ounce package cream cheese, softened

1. Preheat oven to 325°F. Grease and flour cake pan. Set aside.

2. Combine cake mix, butter, and 1 egg. Mix well. Press mixture into baking pan. Combine remaining egg with last two ingredients and spread over top of cake mixture.

3. Bake for 28 minutes. Allow to cool completely in the pan before cutting into squares.

# Friendship Cake

*The friendship cake is a wholesome treat that's perfect to share with people close to your heart. Similar cakes are labor intensive, but this easy recipe gives you more time to focus on friends—and other joys of living.*

**INGREDIENTS | SERVES 12**

1 3.9-ounce box instant vanilla pudding mix

⅔ cup vegetable oil

4 eggs

1 18.25-ounce box yellow cake mix

1½ cups brandied fruit, drained

1 cup chopped pecans

1 cup raisins or golden raisins

Confectioners' sugar

## Original Friendship Cakes

The original version of this cake has a sourdough base. If you're baking it from scratch, you need to factor in the time it takes the sourdough to ferment. This time-consuming step is omitted from this recipe, but the friendship is not. Double the batch and make one cake to enjoy and one to share.

1. Preheat oven to 325ºF. Butter a 12-cup bundt or angel food cake pan and set aside.

2. Combine pudding, oil, eggs, and cake mix in a large mixing bowl and beat for 3 minutes with an electric beater set to medium speed.

3. Gradually add fruit, nuts, and raisins until they are well incorporated into batter. Turn batter into the pan. Bake for 55 minutes.

4. Allow to cool slightly before inverting onto a wire rack to cool. Dust with confectioners' sugar if desired.

# Creamy Coconut Dessert

*What is it that keeps coconut cake on the favorites list? Is it the tropical flavors? The lightness of the whipped topping? The beautiful presentation? The only way to find out is to bake and enjoy this cake—often. Note: Be sure to use pudding that calls for milk.*

**INGREDIENTS | SERVES 8**

1 18.25-ounce box yellow cake mix

2 tablespoons water

1 cup shredded sweetened coconut

1 egg

½ cup butter

1 3.9-ounce package instant lemon pudding plus ingredients called for on box

1 12-ounce tub nondairy whipped topping

1. Preheat oven to 350°F. Grease and flour 9" × 13" cake pan. Set aside.

2. Combine all ingredients except pudding and whipped topping in a large mixing bowl and combine using a wooden spoon.

3. Press dough into pan so that it is evenly distributed and about ¼" thick. Bake for 20 minutes. Allow to cool completely in the pan.

4. Meanwhile, mix lemon pudding according to package instructions.

5. When cake is cool, layer pudding on top of crust. Dollop nondairy whipped topping on top of the pudding.

# Strawberry Shortcake Bake

*Lighter and quicker to bake than traditional shortcakes, this fruity favorite is an everyday dessert that's easy enough to enjoy often. You can use fresh or frozen strawberries.*

## INGREDIENTS | SERVES 8

1 18-ounce box yellow cake mix plus ingredients called for on box

1 5.1-ounce package instant vanilla pudding plus milk called for on box

3 cups strawberries, mashed

1 12-ounce tub nondairy whipped topping

## Shortcakes

Discerning consumers of the shortcake may expect a denser cake under their berries. Adding a bit less pudding can create this effect. Experiment until you reach the texture you like. Don't forget to make notes. There's nothing worse than getting the desired result and forgetting how to re-create it.

1. Prepare and bake cake according to package instructions for two round layer pans. Allow to cool completely.

2. Lay cooled cake layers on a clean, flat surface. Mark the middle of the cake layer with toothpicks. With toothpicks as your guide, slice layer horizontally, using a few slow, even strokes of a serrated knife. Carefully remove top layer to a clean, flat surface. Repeat this process with the second layer to create four layers total.

3. Mix pudding according to instructions on the package. In a large glass bowl, alternate layers of cake, strawberries, and pudding.

4. Top with a generous helping of nondairy whipped topping.

# Sundae Cake

*A great way to enjoy the yummy taste of a sundae without all the dairy. This recipe is just a guideline to get you started. Experiment with your favorite combinations of toppings. Combine flavors. Add fruits. With any luck, this cake will never be the same twice!*

**INGREDIENTS | SERVES 12**

1 18.25-ounce chocolate cake mix plus ingredients called for on box

1 15-ounce tub nondairy whipped topping

3 sliced bananas

1½ cups sliced strawberries

1 14-ounce can crushed pineapple, drained

¼ cup maraschino cherries, drained

4 tablespoons chocolate sauce

1. Prepare and bake cake according to cake mix instructions for a two-layer cake. Sandwich half the whipped topping and all of the fruit pieces between layers of cake.

2. Top with a layer of nondairy whipped topping. Drizzle chocolate sauce over top.

# Chocolate Gooey Cake

*Use this sticky treat to celebrate a great day. This fancy-looking cake is simple enough for an everyday dessert.*

**INGREDIENTS | SERVES 12**

1 18.25-ounce box German chocolate cake plus ingredients called for on box

⅔ cup fudge ice cream topping

¾ cup butterscotch topping

¾ cup sweetened condensed milk

6 chocolate-covered toffee candies

1 15-ounce tub nondairy whipped topping

1. Prepare and bake cake according to cake mix instructions. While cake is still warm in the pan, use a skewer to poke holes all over the top.

2. Pour fudge topping over top of the cake, followed by butterscotch topping and sweetened condensed milk, so that the holes fill with liquid.

3. Place candies in a bag and crush with a rolling pin. Top cake with crushed candies. Frost cake with nondairy whipped topping. Refrigerate until ready to serve.

# Quick Bake Carrot Cake

*This bundt carrot cake is sweet and moist—and may overflow the pan. Bake with a cookie sheet under it to catch drips and dribbles, just in case.*

**INGREDIENTS | SERVES 12**

1 18.25-ounce box carrot cake mix

4 eggs

1½ cups shredded carrots

¾ cup oil

1 cup milk

1 12-ounce tub prepared sour cream frosting

## Frosting Dilemma

To frost or not to frost? That is the question. This cake is so moist and sweet you could almost forgo the frosting, but hardcore fans won't think of it. No worries—just pick up a tub of frosting and slather it on. Enjoy!

1. Preheat oven to 350°F. Grease and flour a 12-cup bundt pan. Set aside.

2. Combine all ingredients except frosting in a large bowl. Mix well until a smooth batter forms. Pour into bundt pan and bake for 55 minutes. Insert a toothpick to check for doneness.

3. Remove cake from oven and allow to cool in the pan for 15 minutes. Invert pan onto wire rack and allow cake to fall free of pan.

4. Allow cake to cool completely before frosting.

# Lemon Goo Cake

*Sure, baking icing into the cake is a little counterintuitive. But this moist, lemony cake is a snap to bake. This cake bakes up very moist and fluffy. Resist testing with a fork or toothpick; the cake can fall easily.*

**INGREDIENTS | SERVES 12**

1 18.25-ounce box lemon cake mix
4 eggs
1 cup milk
1 12-ounce tub lemon frosting

1. Preheat oven to 350°F. Grease and flour 12-cup bundt pan. Set aside.

2. Combine all ingredients in a large mixing bowl. Mix well using an electric mixer set to medium speed to form a smooth batter.

3. Pour into pan and bake for 1 hour. Allow cake to cool slightly before inverting pan onto a wire rack to remove the cake.

# Candied Pumpkin Dessert

*Pumpkins are for more than carving on Halloween. Their buttery texture and sweet flavor make for wholesome desserts when the temperatures drop.*

**INGREDIENTS | SERVES 12**

1 15-ounce can pumpkin (not pumpkin pie filling)
1 12-ounce can evaporated milk
3 eggs
1 cup granulated sugar
4 teaspoons pumpkin pie spice
1 18.25-ounce box white cake mix
¾ cup butter, melted

1. Preheat oven to 350°F. Grease and flour 9" × 13" pan. Set aside.

2. Mix pumpkin, evaporated milk, eggs, sugar, and pumpkin pie spice in a large bowl. Turn mixture into pan. Top with dry cake mix.

3. Pour melted butter on top. Bake 55 minutes. Remove from oven and serve warm.

# Playful Sprinkles Cake

*Sprinkles are a no-effort way to add a little something special to a cake.*
*The playful colors in the cake mix combo make this cake a winner.*

**INGREDIENTS | SERVES 12**

1 18.25-ounce box confetti cake mix

1 12-ounce tub prepared icing with sprinkles

1 cup milk

4 eggs

### Your Cake Pan Overfloweth?

Recipes with icing in the mix are famous for overflowing. To be on the safe side, always keep a cookie sheet (or two) on the rack below your cake. That'll keep drippings off your oven floor and cut down on cleaning time for you!

1. Preheat oven to 350°F. Grease and flour 12-cup bundt pan. Set aside.

2. Combine all ingredients in a large mixing bowl. Mix well using an electric mixer set to medium speed to form a smooth batter.

3. Pour into pan and bake for 1 hour. Allow cake to cool slightly before inverting pan onto a wire rack to remove the cake.

# Peanut Butter Cup Fondue

*This less-formal version of the elegant chocolate fondue sneaks a little protein into the mix. This fondue is served at a cooler temperature, and you can use your fingers to dunk the cake.*

**INGREDIENTS | SERVES 8**

1 18.25-ounce box angel food cake plus ingredients called for on box

1 12-ounce package chocolate morsels

½ cup peanut butter

1. Prepare and bake cake according to cake mix instructions. Cut cake into cubes.

2. Melt chocolate pieces in a double boiler or fondue pot. Stir in peanut butter. Pour into a serving bowl and serve.

# Cantaloupe Squares

*This melon-topped tart boasts a surprising combination of flavors, a lovely texture, and a rich, cream-cheese flavor. Serve in the morning with coffee or at the end of a summer day.*

**INGREDIENTS** | **SERVES 24**

1 18.25-ounce box yellow cake mix
4 eggs, divided
2 tablespoons vegetable oil
16-ounce package cream cheese, softened
⅓ cup granulated sugar
¼ teaspoon salt
1 cup puréed cantaloupe
1 teaspoon vanilla extract
½ cup milk
1 tablespoon lemon juice

1. Preheat oven to 300°F. Grease 9" × 13" pan.

2. Reserve 1 cup cake mix. Mix remaining cake mix, 1 egg, and oil to form a thick batter. Press batter into the pan to form a bottom layer. Set aside.

3. In a large mixing bowl, combine cream cheese, sugar, and salt. Beat with an electric mixer until smooth.

4. Fold in remaining 3 eggs and the 1 cup reserved cake mix. Beat until thoroughly incorporated. Slowly add remaining ingredients and beat until smooth.

5. Pour cheese mixture on top of bottom layer in pan. Bake for 45 minutes or until center is slightly firm to the touch. Remove to refrigerator and chill for 2 hours before serving.

# Raspberry Chocolate Bars

*Raspberry jam and real chocolate chips melt into butter and milk to create a gooey, sweet bar. Added nuts are optional, but they add a rich crunch.*

**INGREDIENTS | SERVES 12**

1 18.25-ounce box chocolate cake mix
⅓ cup evaporated milk
1½ cups melted butter
1 cup chopped nuts (optional)
½ cup seedless raspberry jam
12-ounce chocolate chips

1. Preheat oven to 350°F. Grease and flour 9" × 13" pan. Set aside.

2. Combine cake mix, evaporated milk, butter, and nuts to form a very sticky, gooey batter. Pour half the batter into the bottom of a pan and bake for 10 minutes.

3. Meanwhile, melt the jam in the microwave.

4. Remove baked crust from oven and cover with melted jam and chocolate chips. Cover with remaining cake batter and bake for 20 minutes.

5. Cool completely before cutting.

# Chocolate Cherry Bars

*Enjoy these bars warm out of the oven or cover them and save
them for later. They taste fantastic either way.*

**INGREDIENTS | SERVES 12**

1 18.25-ounce box chocolate cake mix

1 15-ounce can cherry pie filling

1 teaspoon almond extract

1 teaspoon vanilla extract

2 eggs

1 cup sugar

7 tablespoons butter

⅓ cup whole milk

1 12-ounce package semisweet
chocolate chips

1. Preheat oven to 350°F. Spray a 13" × 9" pan with
   nonstick spray. Set aside.

2. Combine cake mix, pie filling, extracts, and eggs in a
   large bowl and beat with an electric mixer until well
   blended.

3. Pour batter into pan and bake at 350°F for 25 minutes
   or until set all the way through. Remove from oven.

4. Mix sugar, butter, and milk in a large saucepan. Bring
   to a boil. Remove pan from heat and add chocolate
   chips, stirring as they melt.

5. Pour chocolate mixture over warm cake and spread to
   cover. Allow to cool and harden before cutting into
   bars.

# Chocolate Fondue

*This elegant classic is a dessert you can dip. Fondue is easy to make and fun to eat, but it does require some equipment. Small children will need to be closely supervised.*

**INGREDIENTS** | **SERVES 8**

1 18.25-ounce box angel food cake mix plus ingredients called for on box

16 ounces dark chocolate

1½ cups half-and-half

1 teaspoon vanilla extract

1. Prepare and bake cake according to cake mix instructions. Cut cake into cubes.

2. Break chocolate into small pieces and place in fondue pot. Gently add half-and-half and stir until melted and smooth. Add vanilla.

3. When melted and mixed, sauce is ready for dipping.

# Yellow Cake Dessert

*Four favorites combine for a sweet dessert offering layers of creamy flavor. It's perfect to pass at potlucks and family dinners.*

**INGREDIENTS** | **SERVES 8**

1 18.25-ounce box yellow cake mix

2 tablespoons water

1 cup coconut

1 egg

½ cup butter, melted

1 3.9-ounce package lemon pudding plus milk called for on box

1 15-ounce tub whipped topping

1. Preheat oven to 350°F. Grease and flour 9" × 13" pan. Set aside.

2. In a large bowl, mix cake mix, water, coconut, egg, and butter using a wooden spoon.

3. Spoon mixture into pan and even out with flat side of a spoon. Bake for 20 minutes. Cool completely.

4. Prepare lemon pudding as directed on box and spread on cooled cake. Top with whipped topping.

# Ricotta Cake

*Somewhere between lemon cake and cheesecake, this recipe finds the perfect balance of richness and sweetness. Topped with confectioners' sugar, it's hard to resist.*

**INGREDIENTS | SERVES 10**

1 18.25-ounce box lemon cake mix with pudding plus ingredients called for on box

1 pound ricotta cheese

¾ cup sugar

3 eggs

Confectioners' sugar

1. Preheat oven to 350°F. Grease and flour cake pan. Set aside.

2. Prepare batter according to cake mix instructions and turn into cake pan. Mix cheese, sugar, and eggs and spoon on top of batter in cake pan. Bake for 50 minutes.

3. Sift confectioners' sugar on top of cake to finish.

# Banana Bread

*Freeze overripe bananas (in the peel) and save them to use in recipes like this one. The peel will turn black when frozen, but the fruit will be great for baking when thawed.*

**INGREDIENTS | SERVES 8**

¼ cup sour cream

1 teaspoon baking soda

Water

1 18.25-ounce box yellow cake mix without pudding

2 eggs

1 cup mashed bananas

1 cup walnuts or walnut pieces

1. Preheat oven to 350°F. Grease and flour cake pan. Set aside.

2. Mix sour cream and baking soda in a 1 cup measuring cup. Add water to 1-cup level and pour mixture into a large mixing bowl.

3. Fold cake mix into sour cream mixture, mixing well. Slowly add eggs, bananas, and nuts.

4. Pour into a loaf pan and bake according to cake mix instructions.

# Chocolate Toffee Shortbread

*This delicious shortbread can be made with any flavor cake mix. If you want to use white or yellow cake mix, use 1 cup of white chocolate chips, ground, in place of the semisweet.*

**INGREDIENTS | YIELDS 48 COOKIES**

1 18.25-ounce package chocolate cake mix

1 12-ounce package semisweet chocolate chips, divided

½ cup butter, softened

1 3-ounce package cream cheese, softened

1 egg

1 teaspoon vanilla

1 cup toffee baking bits

1 cup chopped pecans

1. Preheat oven to 375°F. In large bowl, place cake mix. Grind 1 cup of the chocolate chips in a food processor until fine; stir into cake mix.

2. Add butter, cream cheese, egg, and vanilla to cake mix and mix until a crumbly dough forms.

3. Press dough into 15" × 10" jelly roll pan. Sprinkle with toffee baking bits, pecans, and remaining 1 cup chocolate chips.

4. Bake for 15–20 minutes until shortbread is set. Cool on wire rack, then cut or break into squares. Store in airtight container.

## About Shortbread

Shortbreads traditionally don't use leavening agents. But cake mixes include baking powder or baking soda, so the dough will puff up slightly. Lots of fat, in the form of butter or cream cheese, will help keep the dough from puffing too much.

# Lemon Crunch Cake

*This elegant cake is easy to make, and it serves a crowd.*
*Look for different types of nut brittle to vary the recipe.*

**INGREDIENTS | SERVES 16**

1 18.25-ounce package lemon cake mix
½ cup buttermilk
¼ cup water
½ cup butter, melted
1 teaspoon lemon extract
3 eggs
2 tablespoons lemon juice
2 16-ounce cans ready to spread vanilla frosting
¼ cup lemon juice
1½ cups powdered sugar
1 8-ounce package peanut brittle, crushed

1. Preheat oven to 325°F. Spray a 10" tube pan with nonstick baking spray containing flour and set aside.

2. In large bowl, combine cake mix, buttermilk, water, melted butter, lemon extract, eggs, and 2 tablespoons lemon juice; beat until combined. Then beat 3 minutes at medium speed; pour into prepared pan.

3. Bake for 50–60 minutes or until cake springs back when lightly touched in center. Cool completely on wire rack.

4. In medium bowl, combine frosting with lemon juice and powdered sugar; beat until fluffy. Remove cake from pan and cut horizontally into four layers.

5. Reassemble cake, using frosting, sprinkling each layer with some of the crushed brittle. Cover and let stand for 3–4 hours before serving.

# Lemon Crème Cake

*Pockets of pie filling add a sweet, sensual surprise to this simple dessert. And you don't need a pastry bag or any tricky techniques to whip up this weeknight dessert.*

**INGREDIENTS** | **SERVES 12**

1 18.25-ounce box white cake mix plus ingredients called for on box

1 19-ounce can lemon pie filling

1 12-ounce tub prepared sour cream icing

1 15-ounce tub nondairy whipped topping

## Flavor Combinations

Feel free to switch out cake mix and pie filling flavors with this recipe. White cake and peach pie filling or chocolate cake and cherry filling are great options—but they're only the beginning. Let your imagination go!

1. Preheat oven to 350ºF. Grease and flour 9" × 13" pan. Set aside.

2. Mix batter according to package instructions and pour into pan. Spoon pie filling on top of cake batter in evenly spaced dollops.

3. Bake according to package instructions. As cake bakes, mix together frosting and whipped topping. Allow cake to cool before frosting.

# Sweet Potato Cake

*Nutritionists will tell you that a sweet potato is one of the best things for curbing a sweet tooth. Your first thought may be to run toward the chocolate, but sweet potato is the one that truly satisfies.*

**INGREDIENTS | SERVES 12**

1 18.25-ounce box white cake mix

1 3.9-ounce package vanilla pudding mix (not instant)

1 teaspoon cinnamon

½ teaspoon nutmeg

1⅔ cups cooked sweet potatoes, mashed

4 eggs, beaten

½ cup oil

1 12-ounce tub prepared cream cheese frosting

1. Preheat oven to 350°F. Spray a 13" × 9" pan with nonstick spray. Set aside.

2. Sift together cake mix, pudding, cinnamon, and nutmeg. In a separate bowl mix potatoes, eggs, and oil.

3. Slowly add wet ingredients to dry and mix until a smooth batter forms. Bake for 40 minutes. Cool completely before frosting.

## CHAPTER 5

# Savory Surprises

# Sweet Tooth Cornbread Cake

*This sweeter cornbread makes an old timey treat crumbled in a cold glass of milk or served alongside a spicy stew. Slightly sweet breads ease the bite of an extra-spicy dish.*

**INGREDIENTS | SERVES 6**

5 tablespoons butter

1 cup frozen sweet corn

1 cup whole milk

2 eggs

1 egg yolk

1 teaspoon vanilla

1 8.5-ounce package corn muffin mix

1 9-ounce package yellow cake mix

¼ cup granulated sugar

Confectioners' sugar

1. Preheat oven to 350°F.

2. Slowly melt butter in a 10" cast iron skillet. Add corn and remove skillet from heat.

3. In a large mixing bowl, combine milk, 2 eggs, 1 egg yolk, and vanilla. Mix well until smooth. Fold in corn mix, cake mix, and granulated sugar.

4. Pour mixture over corn and butter in skillet. Bake for 35 minutes. Allow cake to cool for 15 minutes. Invert pan over wire rack or serving plate.

5. Dust with confectioners' sugar if desired or serve with butter.

# Cornbread Croutons

*These sweet and wholesome crunchy bits are fantastic in a salad, floating on a soup, or used in a favorite stuffing recipe at Thanksgiving.*

**INGREDIENTS** | **MAKES 6 CUPS FINISHED CROUTONS**

¼ cup olive oil

Salt and pepper to taste

Herbs to taste

1 recipe Sweet Tooth Cornbread Cake (page 68)

## Storing Croutons

These tiny toasts will keep for a few weeks in a sealed plastic bag. If you want to save them for a special occasion, pop them in the freezer. They'll easily thaw when you're ready to use them.

1. Preheat oven to 350°F.

2. Pour ¼ cup olive oil in a shallow dish. Mix in salt, pepper, and herbs. Cut cornbread into cubes and place on cookie sheet. Lightly brush with the seasoned oil.

3. Bake 8 minutes. Remove croutons from oven and turn with spatula. Return to the oven and bake for another 8 minutes.

4. Allow croutons to cool completely before serving.

# Ham, Beans, and Cornbread

*This slow cooked meal is a Southern style treat and a weeknight favorite waiting to happen.*

**INGREDIENTS** | **SERVES 6**

1 pound dried great northern beans, soaked overnight according to package instructions

½ pound chopped, cooked ham

½ cup brown sugar

1 tablespoon onion powder

1 tablespoon garlic salt

½ teaspoon black pepper

¼ teaspoon cayenne pepper

1 recipe Sweet Tooth Cornbread Cake batter (page 68), unbaked

1. Combine all ingredients except Sweet Tooth Cornbread Cake batter in a slow cooker and add water to cover by 2 inches.

2. Set slow cooker to low and simmer for 10½ hours, stirring occasionally. Add Sweet Tooth Cornbread Cake batter in dollops. Cover and cook for 1½ hours. Ladle into bowls.

# Fruity Brunch Pizza

*Choose fresh fruit in season. Some fruits, like apples and peaches, bake well. You may choose to bake them when you bake the crust. You may choose not to bake others. Get creative with this recipe. The rewards are great!*

**INGREDIENTS** | **SERVES 4**

Refrigerated pizza crust

2 tablespoons butter, melted

½ cup yellow cake mix

¼ cup brown sugar

½ cup vanilla yogurt

Fresh fruit

1. Preheat oven to temperature specified in pizza crust instructions.

2. Lay pizza crust out on a cookie sheet. Baste with butter and sprinkle with cake mix. Sprinkle with brown sugar. Bake according to pizza crust package instructions.

3. Top with a thin layer of vanilla yogurt. Playfully arrange fresh fruit on the pizza for "toppings."

# Dinner Rolls

*These are a perfect complement for a dinner—and a great start for some other exciting recipes. For an irresistible spread, mix honey with your favorite butter or margarine.*

**INGREDIENTS | MAKES 20 ROLLS**

1 0.25-ounce envelope active dry yeast
1½ cups warm water
1 9-ounce package yellow cake mix
3¼ cups flour
¼ cup butter, melted
2 egg whites, beaten

## Dinner Roll Variations

Add the following ingredients in Step 3: For an Italian flavor, add 1 tablespoon mixed Italian herbs, 2 teaspoons crushed garlic, 4 tablespoons grated Parmesan cheese, and 1 tablespoon dried herbs. If you like rosemary, add 3 tablespoons Parmesan cheese and 3 tablespoons finely chopped fresh rosemary or 1 tablespoon dried rosemary. For an autumn twist, add ½ cup dried cranberries and 1 tablespoon pumpkin pie spice mix. For sweet potato rolls, add ½ cup mashed sweet potatoes.

1. Preheat oven to 350°F.

2. In a large mixing bowl dissolve yeast in warm water. Let stand 10 minutes, or until a milky texture appears.

3. Fold in cake mix and flour, beating until a smooth dough forms.

4. Prepare another large mixing bowl with a light coating of spray oil or olive oil.

5. Place dough in oiled bowl, cover with a clean cloth, and leave in a warm place until dough doubles in volume, usually 1 hour. Punch down dough and divide into two halves.

6. Roll out each half into foot-wide circles. Cut each circle into 10 pie-shaped wedges.

7. Brush wedges with melted butter and beaten egg white. Roll each wedge into a crescent shape.

8. Place rolls on a cookie sheet, cover, and let rest for 25 minutes, or until doubled in size. Bake for 12 minutes or until slightly golden.

# Pizza Rolls

*This is a more wholesome take on the pizza rolls you might find in your grocer's freezer.*
*Bake 'em for movie night, but be warned that they won't stick around long.*

**INGREDIENTS | MAKES 20**

1 recipe Dinner Rolls dough (page 71), unbaked
2 tablespoons butter
1½ cups marinara sauce
2 cups shredded mozzarella cheese
40 slices pepperoni

## Variations

Make this with ham and cheese for a great complement to scrambled eggs, or with herbed butter to serve alongside spaghetti or lasagna. Add onions, mushrooms, anchovies, and all of your other favorite pizza toppings to lend a personal touch to this tasty snack.

1. Prepare Dinner Rolls through Step 6. Brush rolls with butter, add a scant spoonful of sauce, some cheese, two pieces of pepperoni, and other toppings as desired.

2. Start at largest side and roll dough toward smallest point to form a crescent shape.

3. Place rolls on a cookie sheet, cover with a clean tea towel, and allow to sit for 25 minutes, or until doubled in size. Bake for 15 minutes or until golden.

4. Allow to cool slightly before serving.

# Peach Pecan Pizza

*Cake mix makes a spicy and delicious crust for this sweet pizza. If you like your desserts spicy, add even more cinnamon, nutmeg, or mace to the cake mix before mixing in the other ingredients.*

**INGREDIENTS | SERVES 8**

1 cup quick cooking oatmeal, divided
1 18.25-ounce package spice cake mix
½ cup butter, softened
1 egg
1 cup chopped toasted pecans, divided
½ teaspoon cinnamon
¼ teaspoon nutmeg
1 21-ounce can peach pie filling
1 cup dried cranberries

## Dessert Pizzas

Dessert pizzas like this one can be varied many ways. Use apple or cherry pie filling instead of peach, and use dried cherries or raisins. A different type of cake mix will also change the flavor. This pizza is good for a dessert or for a fancy brunch.

1. Preheat oven to 350°F. In food processor, grind half of the oatmeal into fine crumbs. Combine the ground oatmeal with cake mix in large bowl; mix well. In same processor bowl, combine cream cheese with butter; process until well blended.

2. Cut butter mixture into cake mix mixture until crumbly. Remove 1 cup of these crumbs and place in small bowl. Add egg to remaining crumbs and mix. Press mixture with egg into greased 13" × 9" cake pan. Bake for 10 minutes.

3. Add remaining ½ cup oatmeal and pecans to reserved 1 cup crumbs. Place pie filling in small bowl; stir in dried cranberries, cinnamon, and nutmeg. Spoon evenly over baked crust. Top with pecan mixture.

4. Bake for 20–25 minutes longer until crumbs are golden brown. Let cool for 30 minutes, then cut into squares to serve.

# Mexican Chili Pie

*Craving a little something spicy for supper? This dish combines sweet
cornbread, spicy chili, and creamy cheese in one simple casserole.*

**INGREDIENTS | SERVES 6**

1 1.25-ounce package McCormick Chili
Seasoning Mix

1 pound lean ground beef or turkey

1 14½-ounce can diced tomatoes,
undrained

1 15-ounce can kidney or pinto beans,
undrained

1 9-ounce box yellow cake mix

1 9-ounce package cornbread mix

2 eggs

⅓ cup milk

½ cup water

2 cups Cheddar cheese, grated

1. Preheat oven to 350°F. Grease a 9" × 13" baking dish.

2. Combine chili seasoning mix, ground meat, tomatoes,
   and beans and cook according to directions on
   envelope. While chili simmers, mix cake mix,
   cornbread mix, eggs, milk, and water in a separate
   bowl.

3. Pour chili into a 9" × 13" baking dish. Top with
   cornbread mixture and sprinkle liberally with
   Cheddar cheese. Bake for 30 minutes or until crust is
   golden.

# Sweet Potato Fritters

*This sweet treat can be served alongside a meal or dusted with confectioners' sugar for dessert. Delicious with aioli or mayonnaise as a savory side.*

**INGREDIENTS | SERVES 4**

1 cup sweet potato, grated

1 cup white cake mix, sifted

1 egg, beaten

½ cup milk

2 cups oil for frying

In a large bowl mix all ingredients well to form a batter. Drop by large spoonfuls into hot oil. Fry for approximately 20 seconds on each side. Lift out browned fritters and drain on a paper towel.

# Spoon Bread Casserole

*This easy-to-bake take on a traditional and butter-drenched Southern favorite is a great dish for potlucks and family gatherings.*

**INGREDIENTS | SERVES 4**

1 cup butter, melted

2 cans whole kernel corn, drained

2 12-ounce cans cream style corn

2 cups sour cream

4 eggs, beaten

1 9-ounce package corn muffin mix

1 9-ounce package yellow cake mix

1. Preheat oven to 375°F.

2. Grease a 3-quart casserole dish. Pour butter and both kinds of corn into dish. Fold in sour cream. Add eggs and both mixes, stirring to combine thoroughly. Bake for 35 minutes.

# Beef Pot Pie

*This warm, nourishing comfort food is a true one-pot meal. Use leftover rolls, lean ground beef, and delicious veggies to make a home-baked supper.*

**INGREDIENTS | SERVES 4**

1½ pounds ground beef

1 onion, chopped

1 15-ounce jar Alfredo sauce

2 cups frozen corn

1 cup frozen green beans

1 cup chopped tomatoes, fresh or canned

1 teaspoon dried basil

½ recipe Dinner Rolls dough (page 71), unbaked

1 tablespoon grated Parmesan cheese

¼ teaspoon oregano

1. Preheat oven to 400°F. Lightly grease a 2-quart baking dish and set aside.

2. In a large skillet, brown ground beef and onion. Add Alfredo sauce, corn, beans, tomatoes, and basil. Bring to a boil. Pour mixture into baking dish.

3. Dot beef mixture with Dinner Rolls dough. Sprinkle with Parmesan cheese and oregano. Bake for 15 minutes or until bread topping is golden brown.

# Scalloped Corn Casserole

*If you like corn pudding, give this savory take a try. This rich, creamy corn casserole is fantastic with ham or roast chicken.*

**INGREDIENTS | SERVES 3**

2 eggs

1 cup sour cream

½ cup butter, melted

1 12-ounce can creamed corn

1 12-ounce can whole kernel corn, undrained

1 9-ounce package yellow cake mix

1 cup shredded Cheddar cheese

1. Preheat oven to 350°F. Lightly grease a 9" × 9" baking dish.

2. Lightly beat eggs. Fold in sour cream, butter, and both kinds of corn. Mix well. Fold in cake mix. Spoon into baking dish. Top with shredded cheese.

3. Bake for 55 minutes or until center is set.

# Breakfast Bake Casserole

*This sweet and savory morning treat is easy to make as long as there's a steaming cup of coffee at your side.*

**INGREDIENTS** | **SERVES 6**

2 cups yellow cake mix, divided

8 slices bacon, cooked

1 4-ounce can sliced mushrooms, drained

2 green onions, thinly sliced

1½ cups shredded mild Cheddar cheese

4 eggs

2 cups whole milk

½ cup butter

1. Sprinkle 1 cup cake mix in the bottom of a well-buttered 8" square baking dish. Top with bacon, mushrooms, onions, and cheese. Sprinkle with remaining cake mix.

2. In a medium bowl, whisk together eggs and milk. Pour over layered ingredients. Refrigerate at least 1 hour, preferably overnight.

3. Dot with butter and bake, uncovered, for 1 hour or until center is set.

# Sweetest Hushpuppies

*Serve these round treats at your next fish fry for a sweeter savory crunch. Dip in tartar sauce or ketchup or sprinkle with malt vinegar for an extra burst of flavor.*

**INGREDIENTS** | **MAKES 24 HUSHPUPPIES**

1 9-ounce package cornbread mix

1 9-ounce package yellow cake mix

2 eggs

4 teaspoons baking powder

1 teaspoon salt

1 large onion, finely chopped

¼ cup milk

Oil for frying

1. Combine all ingredients except milk and oil. Mix to form a crumbly mixture. Add milk and stir to form a batter. Drop by teaspoons into 1 inch hot oil in a 12" skillet.

2. Cook until golden on both sides. Remove from oil and let drain on paper towels. Serve warm.

# Hamburger Cornbread Casserole

*This wholesome and easy-to-bake savory recipe will warm you up on a chilly evening. Serve with a salad or green beans for a well-balanced meal.*

**INGREDIENTS | SERVES 6**

2 pounds ground beef
1 yellow onion, chopped
1 14½-ounce can tomato sauce
2 12-ounce cans sweet corn, drained
2 tablespoons chili powder
1 9-ounce package cornbread mix
1 9-ounce package yellow cake mix
2 eggs
⅓ cup milk
⅓ cup water

1. Preheat oven to 350°F. Grease a 9" × 13" pan.

2. Brown ground beef and onion. Drain fat. Add tomato sauce, corn, and chili powder to skillet and sauté for 10 minutes to release the spice.

3. Mix the cornbread mix and cake mix. Add eggs, milk, and water. Beat until a smooth batter forms, adding more water if needed.

4. Spread hamburger and onion mixture in greased pan. Pour cornbread mixture over top. Bake 20–30 minutes or until crust is golden.

# Sweet Potato Casserole

*This dish is delicious enough for the Thanksgiving table but easy enough for an average Thursday night. This easy-to-make recipe brings wholesome goodness to the table.*

**INGREDIENTS** | **SERVES 6**

3 cups mashed sweet potatoes

3 cups granulated sugar

1 cup butter

2 eggs

1 teaspoon vanilla

⅓ cup milk

1 cup sweetened shredded coconut

1 cup brown sugar

1 cup white cake mix

1 cup pecans

1. Preheat oven to 350°F.

2. Mix sweet potatoes, sugar, ½ cup melted butter, eggs, vanilla, milk, and coconut in a large mixing bowl with a wooden spoon. Pour into a buttered baking dish.

3. In a smaller mixing bowl, mix brown sugar, cake mix, and pecans. Sprinkle dry mixture over potatoes. Dot evenly with remaining butter. Bake for 25 minutes.

# CHAPTER 6

# Morning Glory Cakes

# Rich Topped Coffee Cake

*This moist, rich coffee cake makes any coffee klatch a special occasion. Serve with a side of fresh blueberries or creamy yogurt for a lovely full breakfast.*

### INGREDIENTS | SERVES 6

1 18.25-ounce box yellow cake mix
1 3.9-ounce box instant vanilla pudding
1 cup sour cream
4 whole eggs
½ cup canola oil
½ cup skim milk
3 teaspoons ground cinnamon
¼ cup sugar
1 tablespoon flour

1. Preheat oven to 350°F.

2. Mix cake mix and vanilla pudding mix in a bowl. Add sour cream, oil, and milk. Lightly beat eggs and fold into mixture. Blend using electric mixer on medium speed for 10 minutes. Pour into an angel food pan or bundt pan.

3. In a separate bowl combine cinnamon, sugar, and flour. Pour into pan on top of cake mix mixture.

4. Use a knife to cut through batter at intervals to marble topping through batter. Bake for 50 minutes or until knife comes out clean. Serve with coffee.

# Citrus Muffins

*The bright, sparkling taste of orange makes this fresh and sweet morning treat perfect for days at the beach house, by the pool, or with friends.*

### INGREDIENTS | MAKES 24 MUFFINS

1 18.25-ounce box white cake mix
1 cup water
2 eggs
1 16-ounce box confectioners' sugar
Zest of 1 orange
Juice and zest of 2 lemons

1. Preheat oven to 325°F. Butter and flour a muffin tin.

2. Blend cake mix, water, and eggs with an electric mixer for 4 minutes. Fill muffin cups ½ full with batter. Bake for 6 minutes.

3. Meanwhile, combine confectioners' sugar, orange zest, and lemon zest and juice to make a glaze. Set aside.

4. Remove muffins from oven. Let cool on rack. When only slightly warm to touch, dip the top of each muffin in glaze to cover. Return to rack.

# Cake Mix Pancakes

*This is less of a recipe and more of a trick. But it's a great one to know! With this in your toolbox you can whip up some surprising and yummy pancakes on short notice any day of the week!*

**INGREDIENTS | 12 PANCAKES**

1 18.25-ounce box cake mix plus
  ingredients called for on box
½ cup butter or ¼ cup oil for frying

## Get Creative

Don't be afraid to toss fruit, nuts, or even bits of candy bar into the mix on very special occasions. Make banana bread pancakes with walnuts and real maple syrup on top, white cake mix pancakes with blueberries and blueberry syrup, cherry cake mix pancakes with chocolate syrup, confetti cake mix pancakes for a birthday, and pineapple cake mix pancakes with blueberry syrup. Have fun!

1. Make cake mix batter according to package directions. Melt 1 tablespoon butter or heat ½ tablespoon oil in a skillet or griddle. Ladle ¼ cup pancake batter per pancake into skillet.

2. Flip when bubbles form on top of pancakes. Serve with fresh fruit, syrup, and/or whipped cream!

# Better Buttermilk Breakfast Cake

*Rich, sweet buttermilk cake for breakfast. Sounds too sweet to be true, doesn't it? Well, hold on to your sweet tooth! This morning treat is all dolled up and headed for a plate near you.*

**INGREDIENTS | SERVES 8**

1 18.25-ounce box white cake mix

1 cup plus 1 tablespoon buttermilk, divided

½ cup plus 1 tablespoon melted butter, divided

5 eggs

3 tablespoons brown sugar

2 teaspoons ground cinnamon

1 tablespoon granulated sugar

1 cup finely chopped nuts

1 cup confectioners' sugar

1 teaspoon vanilla extract

1. Preheat oven to 350°F. Grease a 10" tube pan.

2. Combine cake mix, 1 cup buttermilk, and ½ cup melted butter. Mix using an electric mixer set to medium speed for 2 minutes. Add eggs and continue beating.

3. In a separate bowl, mix brown sugar and cinnamon.

4. Sprinkle granulated sugar and nuts into bottom of tube pan. Pour in one-third of the batter. Sprinkle batter with brown sugar mixture. Top with remaining batter. Bake for 45 minutes.

5. Remove cake from oven and cool in pan for 15 minutes. Invert pan onto serving surface and let cool an additional 30 minutes.

6. Meanwhile, mix confectioners' sugar, vanilla extract, the remaining 1 tablespoon buttermilk, and the remaining 1 tablespoon melted butter to form a glaze. When cake has cooled, drizzle with glaze.

# Chocolate Cheese Muffins

*Chocolate, cream cheese, and crunchy walnuts work together
to make this home-baked muffin a sweet, rich favorite.*

**INGREDIENTS** | **MAKES 24 MUFFINS**

1 18.25-ounce box chocolate cake mix
  plus ingredients called for on box

1 8-ounce package cream cheese,
  softened

¼ cup sugar

1 egg

1 cup chocolate chips

½ cup chopped walnuts

1 16-ounce container cream cheese
  frosting

1. Preheat oven to 350°F. Grease muffin tin or line with paper cups. Set aside.

2. Prepare cake batter according to package instructions. Fill muffin cups ½ full.

3. In a separate bowl, mix cream cheese, sugar, and egg until fluffy. Fold in chocolate chips and walnuts. Mix evenly.

4. Drop a heaping teaspoon of the cream cheese mixture into the center of the batter in each muffin cup. Bake muffins for 15 to 20 minutes. Remove from oven and cool completely.

5. Frost cooled muffins with cream cheese frosting.

# Easy as Apple Pie Muffins

*These warm delicious muffins are surprisingly easy to make. With just
five ingredients, they're easy to whip up almost any day.*

**INGREDIENTS** | **MAKES 24 MUFFINS**

2 large eggs

1 cup sour cream

1 21-ounce can apple pie filling

1 18.25-ounce box spice cake mix

Optional: Freshly ground cinnamon

1. Preheat oven to 350°F. Grease muffin tin or line with paper baking cups. Set aside.

2. Mix eggs, sour cream, and apple pie filling in a bowl with a wooden spoon. Gently fold in cake mix. Do not overmix. Fill muffin cups ½ full.

3. Sprinkle with cinnamon if desired. Bake for 25 minutes. Cool in pan. When cool enough to touch, remove from pan. Serve slightly warm with real butter.

### Baking Apples

Fuji, Gala, Braeburn, Jonathan, McIntosh, Newton Pippin, Rome Beauty, and Winesap apples are generally considered best for baking, but you can try any apple you like. If you find one you like, make a note of when they're in season—that way you can make this cake a yearly tradition.

# Lemon Poppyseed Muffins

*Lemon Poppyseed Muffins are a coffeehouse favorite that are easy to make at home. Adding a few extra ingredients to lemon cake mix makes for some sweet sailing.*

**INGREDIENTS  |  MAKES 24 MUFFINS**

1 18.25-ounce box lemon cake mix

2 tablespoons flour

3 eggs

⅔ cup milk

⅓ cup vegetable oil

1 teaspoon baking powder

2 tablespoons poppyseeds

1. Preheat oven to 375ºF. Grease muffin tin or line with paper cups. Set aside.

2. Mix all ingredients in a large mixing bowl using an electric mixer set to medium speed. Fill muffin cups ½ full. Bake for 20 minutes or until tops are golden.

3. Serve warm.

# Warm Spice Muffins

*The comforting blend of spices in the batter are heightened with an extra sprinkle of cinnamon. What could be better on a cozy morning?*

**INGREDIENTS  |  MAKES 24 MUFFINS**

1 18.25-ounce box spice cake mix

2 tablespoons flour

3 eggs

⅔ cup milk

⅓ cup vegetable oil

1 teaspoon baking powder

2 tablespoons each cinnamon and sugar
  to garnish

1. Preheat oven to 375ºF. Grease muffin tin or line with paper cups and set aside.

2. Mix all ingredients except cinnamon and sugar in a large mixing bowl using an electric mixer set to medium speed. Fill muffin cups ½ full.

3. Sprinkle cinnamon and sugar on top of each muffin. Bake for 20 minutes or until tops are golden. Serve warm.

# Raspberry Muffins

*Love sweets in the morning? This recipe creates a treat that's really a cake masquerading as a muffin. Sweet berries and aromatic vanilla make for a lovely start to the morning.*

**INGREDIENTS | MAKES 24 MUFFINS**

1 18.25-ounce box French vanilla cake mix
2 tablespoons flour
3 eggs
⅔ cup milk
⅓ cup vegetable oil
1 teaspoon baking powder
1 cup raspberries

1. Preheat oven to 375°F. Grease muffin tin or line with paper baking cups. Set aside.

2. Mix all ingredients in a large mixing bowl using an electric mixer set to medium speed. Fill muffin cups ½ full. Bake for 20 minutes or until tops are golden.

3. Serve warm.

# Toasty Blueberry Loaf

*This really is the best thing since sliced bread! It's great for a group or for traveling. Simply bake, wrap in foil, and you're good to go!*

**INGREDIENTS | SERVES 12**

2 large eggs
1 cup sour cream
1 21-ounce can blueberry pie filling
1 18.25-ounce box white cake mix
Sugar for dusting

1. Preheat oven to 350°F. Grease loaf pans and set aside.

2. Mix eggs, sour cream, and blueberry pie filling in a bowl with a wooden spoon. Gently fold in cake mix. Do not overmix. Fill loaf pans halfway with batter.

3. Sprinkle with sugar to taste. Bake for 25 minutes. Cool in pan. When cool enough to touch, remove from pan. Slice and serve.

# Blueberry Muffin French Toast

*This day-after recipe is the perfect way to use up any leftover slices of blueberry loaf.*
*In fact, a night on the counter gives the flavors time to blend.*

**INGREDIENTS | SERVES 6**

1 Toasty Blueberry Loaf (page 88), baked
2 eggs, beaten
1 cup corn flakes, crumbled
Butter for frying
Blueberry syrup
Whipped topping (optional)

1. Dredge slices of Toasty Blueberry Loaf through egg. Roll in corn flakes to coat. Fry slices in butter until golden and transfer to plate immediately.

2. Serve warm with blueberry syrup and a dollop of whipped topping.

### Toasting Tips

If you're working with thicker slices of muffin loaf, allow the slices to soak for 15 seconds in the egg batter. The egg will have just a little more time to incorporate into the muffin so you'll have a slightly firmer consistency when it's cooked.

# Super-Easy Fruity Muffins

*This recipe is unbelievably simple. The secret to success is choosing*
*the right cake mix flavor and fruit combination. Be creative!*

**INGREDIENTS | MAKES 24 MUFFINS**

1 12-ounce can unsweetened fruit, drained
1 18.25-ounce box cake mix

1. Preheat oven to 350°F. Grease muffin tin or line with paper baking cups. Set aside.

2. Gently stir fruit into mix to form a thick, lumpy batter. Fill muffin cups ½ full. Bake for 30 minutes or until a toothpick comes out clean.

3. Serve warm with sour cream or butter.

# Banana-Nut Muffins

*Banana-nut has been a flavor favorite for generations. There's something about the combination of smooth fruit and crunchy nuts that keeps us coming back for more!*

**INGREDIENTS** | **MAKES 24 MUFFINS**

1 18.25-ounce box butter pecan cake mix

1 3.9-ounce package instant banana pudding

4 eggs

2 bananas, mashed

½ cup vegetable oil

½ cup water

1 teaspoon banana extract

¾ teaspoon ground cinnamon

1 cup finely chopped walnuts

1. Preheat oven to 350°F. Grease muffin tin or line with paper baking cups. Set aside.

2. Mix all ingredients except nuts in a large bowl until smooth. Fold in nuts with a wooden spoon. Fill muffin cups or loaf pans ¾ full.

3. Bake for 20 minutes or until toothpick comes out clean. Serve warm with butter.

## Ripe Bananas

Have ripe bananas before you're ready to bake? Simply peel them, cut them into chunks, wrap them in plastic wrap, and pop them in the freezer. This way, when baking day rolls around all you'll need to do is defrost them and toss them in the batter.

# Healthier Brownie Muffins

*This recipe is a secret weapon for the health-minded baker.*
*It's a chocolaty way to sneak some fiber into your day.*

**INGREDIENTS | MAKES 24 MUFFINS**

3 cups bran cereal
2¼ cups water
1 package low-fat brownie mix
1½ teaspoons baking powder

## Shopping for Bran Cereal

Every box in the cereal aisle touts some sort of health benefits. Many are fortified with vitamins, dehydrated fruits, or—less healthy—tiny marshmallows. Look for whole-grain cereals that are high in fiber. Make these a part of your daily diet and you could see a more stabilized blood sugar level as well as lower cholesterol.

1. Preheat oven to 350°F. Line muffin tin with paper baking cups.

2. In a small bowl, soak cereal in the water for 5 minutes. Then, in a separate and larger bowl, mix soaked cereal, brownie mix, and baking powder till a moist batter forms.

3. Fill up each cupcake cup to the brim. Bake for 25 minutes. Serve with butter.

# Sweet Bran Muffins

*Orange and vanilla give this basic bran muffin a little extra something sweet!*
*For those with a sweet tooth, it's a lovely start to the morning.*

**INGREDIENTS | MAKES 24 MUFFINS**

2 cups 40% bran cereal
1¼ cups hot milk
2 tablespoons oil
1 egg
1 18.25-ounce box yellow cake mix
½ teaspoon vanilla extract
¼ teaspoon orange extract
2 tablespoons butter, melted

1. Preheat oven to 400°F. Generously butter muffin pan.

2. Mix cereal and hot milk in a large mixing bowl and let mixture rest for 10 minutes. Use an electric beater set to high speed to mix oil and egg and extracts into cereal and milk.

3. Use a wooden spoon to fold in cake mix. Mix gently until batter is wet. Do not overmix. It's okay if this batter is a little lumpy.

4. Cover the bowl with a tea towel and let batter rest for 20 minutes. Spoon batter into muffin pan. Bake for 25 minutes.

5. Remove from oven and brush with butter. Let cool before serving.

# Sweet Rolls

*These are the perfect rolls to serve with homemade jam and butter. In autumn, serve with apple butter for a side that celebrates the season. This also makes a great side for good old bacon and eggs.*

**INGREDIENTS | MAKES 24 ROLLS**

1 18.25-ounce box white cake mix
2 0.25-ounce packages active dry yeast
5 cups all-purpose flour
2½ cups hot water
2 tablespoons butter, softened
Ground cinnamon
Granulated sugar
½ cup margarine
¼ cup firmly packed brown sugar
¼ cup light corn syrup
1 cup chopped nuts

1. Preheat oven to 375°F.

2. Combine cake mix, yeast, and flour in a large bowl. Mix in hot water. Set aside to rise until dough doubles in size. Cut dough in half.

3. Roll half of dough into a rectangle on a floured surface. Coat with softened butter, then sprinkle with cinnamon and granulated sugar to taste. Roll jellyroll style and cut into 2" slices. Place into a greased baking pan. Repeat with the rest of the dough.

4. Let cut rolls rise in the pan until they've doubled again. Meanwhile, mix margarine, brown sugar, corn syrup, and nuts. Pour nut and syrup mixture over rolls.

5. Bake for 25 minutes. Let cool.

# Cake Doughnuts

*Doughnuts are a treat, but homemade doughnuts are a slice of heaven. If you've never had a homemade doughnut, make sure you change that right away. With a recipe this easy there's no excuse not to!*

**INGREDIENTS** | **MAKES 24 DOUGHNUTS**

1 tablespoon yeast

2 cups warm water

1 18.25-ounce box white cake mix

4 cups flour

2 cups vegetable oil for frying

## Doughnut Glaze

Whisk ¼ cup whole milk and 1 teaspoon vanilla extract in a saucepan over low heat. Sift in 2 cups confectioners' sugar. Remove from heat and submerge pan in a bowl of warm water to keep glaze from hardening.

1. In a large bowl, mix yeast and warm water until yeast is dissolved. Add cake mix and flour. Mix with spoon to make a soft dough. Set aside for 1 hour so dough can rise.

2. With a floured pin, roll dough out onto a flat surface. Cut with a floured biscuit cutter. Remove to flat board or cookie sheet for 30–45 minutes to rise. Meanwhile, prepare glaze.

3. Fry doughnuts in 2 inches of vegetable oil or in mini-deep fryer. If using a skillet, fry doughnuts on each side and remove with a slotted spoon. If using a deep fryer, follow manufacturer's instructions.

4. Set fried doughnuts on a paper towel to drain and cool slightly. Glaze doughnuts before they cool completely. Serve warm.

# Apple Delight Brunch Cake

*Baked apples are one of the homiest smells in the world. Fill your house—*
*and your stomach—with some of the sweetest comfort food around.*

**INGREDIENTS | SERVES 12**

1 18.25-ounce box yellow or butter cake
mix

3 eggs

½ cup butter, softened

⅔ cup water

5 apples, pared, cored, and sliced

3 tablespoons sugar

4 teaspoons ground cinnamon

Confectioners' sugar as desired for
garnish

## Pared Down

Paring apples is easy when you know how
to do it. Consider buying an apple corer.
These handheld devices allow you to cut
the core from the apple before you slice
the flesh and then peel the slices. This may
seem like an extra step, but it'll save you
prep time.

1. Preheat oven to 375°F. Butter and flour a 10" tube pan.
   Set aside.

2. Mix cake mix, eggs, butter, and water in a large bowl.
   Beat with an electric mixer for 2 full minutes. Turn ⅔
   of the batter into the tube pan.

3. In a separate bowl combine apples, sugar, and
   cinnamon. Layer apple mixture on top of batter in
   pan. Pour remaining batter over apples.

4. Bake for 45 minutes or until toothpick comes out
   clean. Invert onto cooling rack without removing pan.
   After 30 minutes, lift pan off of cake. Cool completely.

5. Garnish with powdered sugar. Slice and serve.

# Mandarin Orange Muffins

*Keep these two ingredients on hand in case company stops by—
or you find a little extra time some morning.*

**INGREDIENTS | SERVES 15**

1 18.25-ounce box white cake mix
marked "just add water"
1 12-ounce can mandarin oranges

1. Preheat oven to 350°F. Grease muffin tin or line with paper baking cups. Set aside.

2. Combine cake mix and oranges in a large mixing bowl. Mix until incorporated; do not expect a smooth batter. Fill muffin cups ⅔ full.

3. Bake for 25 minutes.

# Chocolate Waffles

*Who would have thought waffles could get more decadent? This extra-sweet
treat is a delight for late-night gatherings or the morning after a sleepover.*

**INGREDIENTS | SERVES 24**

1 18-ounce box chocolate cake mix, plus
ingredients called for on box
Whipped topping
Fresh strawberries (optional)

1. Mix cake batter according to instructions on the box. Prepare waffle iron and bake waffles according to manufacturer's instructions.

2. Top warm waffles with whipped topping and strawberries.

# Piña Colada Sunrise Muffins

*This tropical sweet gets your morning started right. Serve with a wedge of pineapple or with a tray of fruit and cheese for a morning to remember.*

**INGREDIENTS** | **MAKES 24 MUFFINS**

1 18.25-ounce box yellow cake mix plus ingredients called for on box

1 teaspoon coconut extract

1 teaspoon rum extract

1 cup flaked coconut

½ to 1 cup chopped nuts

1 8-ounce can crushed pineapple, with juice

1. Preheat oven to temperature listed on cake mix box for cupcakes. Grease muffin tins or line with paper liners and set aside.

2. Mix cake batter according to package instructions. Add remaining ingredients. Beat with an electric mixer for exactly 1 minute on low speed.

3. Fill muffin cups ½ full with batter. Bake for amount of time listed on cake mix box for cupcakes. Garnish with a parasol. Serve with coffee and juice.

# Tropical Angel Muffins

*This light, elegant citrus recipe is great on a summer day or with
a cup of hot coffee. Add a side of sweet yogurt.*

**INGREDIENTS | MAKES 24 MUFFINS**

1 16-ounce box fat-free angel food cake
mix
1 14-ounce can crushed pineapple with
juice
1 10-ounce can mandarin oranges, drained
Zest of 1 orange

## Buy Organic

If possible, choose organic citrus fruits for
recipes that require zest. Some conventional citrus growers use waxes or pesticides that become concentrated in the
rinds. Organic options may mean many
fewer toxins and a fresher, cleaner taste.

1. Preheat oven to 350°F. Coat muffin pans with nonstick
   spray. Set aside.

2. Combine cake mix, pineapple and juice, and
   mandarin oranges. Mix well. Gently mix in orange
   zest. Fill each muffin cup ½ full. Bake for 15 minutes.

3. Remove muffins from pan and cool on a rack.

# CHAPTER 7

# Cooking for a Crowd

# Summer on the Patio Cake

*This fruity sheet cake is perfect for a crowd. Get creative with toppings.*
*Peaches, strawberries, and blueberries make beautiful choices.*

**INGREDIENTS | SERVES 12**

1 18.25-ounce box white cake mix plus
  ingredients called for on box

1 8-ounce box cream cheese

1 cup confectioners' sugar

1 teaspoon vanilla

1 15-ounce tub nondairy whipped
  topping

Seasonal fruit

1. Prepare and bake cake according to cake mix instructions. Let cake cool completely.

2. Mix cream cheese, confectioners' sugar, vanilla, and nondairy whipped topping completely. Spread on cooled cake. Arrange fresh fruit on top of topping.

3. Cover and keep cool until ready to serve.

## Freshest Fruit

Fruit looks luscious when you slice it but can wilt and become brown shortly thereafter. To keep it looking plump, fresh, and juicy, consider tossing the cut fruit with a squeeze of fresh lemon juice or a dash of a fruit-preserving product. Either of these will help. However, the best way to ensure that fruit looks fantastic is to slice it as close to serving time as possible.

# Jack Horner's Chocolate Cake

*This moist and generous cake is intended for a truly big crowd. Extended family gatherings, church suppers, and neighborhood picnics are all great reasons to pull this recipe off the shelf.*

**INGREDIENTS | SERVES 48**

1½ pints canned, pitted plums with liquid

2 18-ounce boxes chocolate cake mix

12 egg whites

¼ cup vegetable oil

1 cup chocolate chips

2 tablespoons confectioners' sugar

1. Preheat oven to 350°F. Coat a 26" × 18" × 1" sheet cake pan with cooking spray. Set aside.

2. Reserve plum liquid and purée pitted plums to get 2¼ cups. Add ¾ cup of the reserved plum liquid.

3. In a large bowl, using an electric mixer set to medium speed, mix both boxes of cake mix with plum mixture, egg whites, and oil. Fold in chocolate chips. Pour into cake pan.

4. Bake for 20 minutes. Allow cake to cool completely. Dust with confectioners' sugar.

# Brownies for a Crowd

*Make a large batch of moist, rich, double chocolate brownies for a hungry crowd with a sweet tooth. Just make sure you've got a glass of cold milk for everyone.*

**INGREDIENTS | SERVES 24**

2 3.9-ounce packages chocolate instant pudding mix

4 cups whole milk

2 18.25-ounce packages chocolate cake mix without pudding

4 cups chocolate chips

Confectioners' sugar for garnish

1. Preheat oven to 350°F. Grease and flour two 10" × 15" jellyroll pans. Set aside.

2. In a large bowl, whisk together both boxes of pudding mix and milk. Slowly fold in both boxes of cake mix. Fold in chocolate chips. Bake 35 minutes. Dust with confectioners' sugar.

3. Allow to cool completely before cutting into squares.

# Lemon Sheet Cake

*To add even more of a lemony kick, add a couple teaspoons of lemon zest to the batter before you bake it. Freeze in an airtight container; remove and thaw cake for 5 minutes before serving.*

**INGREDIENTS | SERVES 30**

1 18-ounce box lemon cake mix
4 eggs
1 can lemon pie filling
1 3-ounce package softened cream cheese
1 cup butter, softened
2 cups confectioners' sugar
1½ teaspoons vanilla

1. Preheat oven to 350°F. Coat a 15" × 10" × 1" baking pan with cooking spray. Set aside.

2. Mix the cake mix, eggs, and pie filling to form a smooth batter. Pour batter into pan. Bake for 20 minutes. Cool on a wire rack.

3. While cake cools, mix cream cheese, butter, and confectioners' sugar until smooth. Add vanilla and mix well. Frost the cooled cake. Refrigerate until ready to serve.

# Fruity Cake for a Crowd

*Milk, cheese, and fruit add a wholesome touch to this nourishing, sweet cake. Beautiful to see and easy to serve, it's a go-to recipe for large parties.*

**INGREDIENTS | SERVES 24**

1 18.25-ounce box yellow cake mix plus ingredients called for on box
1½ cups milk
1 8-ounce box cream cheese
1 3.9-ounce box banana-flavored instant pudding
1 can crushed pineapple
6 bananas
Fresh strawberries
1 15-ounce tub whipped topping

1. Preheat oven to 350°F. Grease and flour cake pan. Set aside.

2. Prepare and bake cake according to package instructions. Allow cake to cool completely while you mix the topping.

3. Combine the milk and cream cheese and pudding. Layer on top of cooled cake.

4. Add a layer of pineapple, sliced bananas, and fresh strawberries. Top with whipped topping.

# Get-Together Coffee Cake

*Make sure the first and last layers are batter layers. Sugar can
burn too quickly on an unprotected top layer.*

**INGREDIENTS | SERVES 24**

1 18.25-ounce box yellow cake mix

1 3.9-ounce box instant vanilla pudding
  mix

¾ cup oil

¾ cup water

4 eggs

1 teaspoon vanilla extract

1 teaspoon butter flavoring or extract

1½ cups chopped nuts

1¼ cups sugar

4 teaspoons cinnamon

1. Preheat oven to 350°F. Grease and flour a tube pan.
   Set aside.

2. Mix cake mix, pudding mix, oil, water, eggs, vanilla
   extract, and butter flavoring for 5 minutes using an
   electric mixer set on low speed.

3. In a separate bowl, combine nuts, sugar, and
   cinnamon.

4. Pour ½" layer of cake mix into the pan. Sprinkle a
   layer of nuts and spices on top. Repeat as often as
   needed in order to fill the pan, ending with batter.
   Bake for 50 minutes.

5. Allow cake to cool completely before serving.

# Favorite Potluck Bars

*Consider these for bake sales and other community events. These bars are sweet, tasty, and completely portable. They arrive at your event in style and fly off the plate.*

**INGREDIENTS** | **MAKES 48 BARS**

1 18.25-ounce box white cake mix
2 large eggs
⅓ cup vegetable oil
1 can sweetened condensed milk
1 cup semisweet chocolate chips
Walnuts, peanuts, or coconut to taste
¼ cup butter

1. Preheat oven to 350°F. Butter a 13" × 9" × 2" baking dish. Set aside.

2. Combine cake mix, eggs, and oil in a bowl and beat until evenly mixed. Press ⅔ of the batter in the bottom of the pan.

3. Combine condensed milk, chocolate chips, and butter in a microwave-safe bowl. Microwave for 1 minute on high power. Remove and stir with a fork until smooth.

4. Pour chocolate mixture over crust. Layer nuts or coconut on top of chocolate layer. Dot with remaining cake batter.

5. Bake for 20 minutes or until lightly browned. Let cool in baking dish. Cut into squares and serve.

# Easy Black Forest Cobbler

*When feeding a large crowd, it's a good idea to fall back on familiar
and well-loved flavors like chocolate and cherries.*

**INGREDIENTS | SERVES 24**

1 15-ounce can cherry pie filling
½ cup butter, softened
1 18.25-ounce box chocolate cake mix
Semisweet chocolate chips to taste
Vanilla ice cream or whipped topping

1. Preheat oven to 375°F.

2. Pour cherry pie filling into a greased 9" × 9" cake pan. Set aside.

3. Cut butter into chocolate cake mix until a crumbly mixture forms. Layer cake mixture on top of cherry pie filling. Dot with chocolate chips. Bake for 30 minutes.

4. Allow to cool slightly. Top with ice cream or whipped topping. Serve warm.

# Peach Cobbler

*It's hard to find a simpler recipe that yields a more lovely dish. Prepared filling and boxed batter
mean most of the work has been done for you. All that's left is to bake and enjoy.*

**INGREDIENTS | SERVES 12**

1 15-ounce can peach pie filling
1 18-ounce box spice cake mix
½ cup butter, softened
Vanilla ice cream or whipped topping

1. Preheat oven to 375°F. Grease a 9" × 9" cake pan.

2. Pour peach pie filling into pan. Set aside.

3. Cut butter into spice cake mix until a crumbly mixture forms. Layer cake mixture on top of pie filling. Bake for 30 minutes.

4. Allow to cool slightly. Top with ice cream or whipped topping. Serve warm.

# Cherry Tunnel Cake

*Cherries and cream are a crowd-pleasing combination. Team with a dark cup of coffee for a sweet treat.*

**INGREDIENTS | SERVES 12**

1 18.25-ounce box white cake mix plus ingredients called for on box

1 cup boiling water

1 3-ounce package cherry flavored gelatin

1 21-ounce can cherry pie filling

1 16-ounce tub nondairy whipped topping

1. Preheat oven to 350°F. Grease and flour 9" × 13" cake pan. Set aside.

2. Prepare and bake cake mix according to package instructions for a 9" × 13" cake. After baking, while cake is still warm, use a fork to poke holes in the cake from the top down.

3. Allow cake to cool. Meanwhile, mix water and gelatin. Pour mixture over cake so that it fills in the holes.

4. Seal the top of the cake with a generous layer of cherry pie filling. Frost the cake with whipped topping. Chill cake for at least 1 hour before serving.

# Fuzzy Navel Cake

*Allow two days for this cake. It's not complicated, but some of the ingredients need to sit overnight.*

**INGREDIENTS** | **SERVES 12**

1 16-ounce can sliced cling peaches with liquid

½ cup peach schnapps

1 cup sugar

1 18.25-ounce package yellow cake mix

1 3.9-ounce package instant vanilla pudding

4 eggs

⅔ cup oil

1 cup chopped pecans

1⅓ cups confectioners' sugar

1. Drain peaches and reserve liquid. Chop peaches. Combine peaches, schnapps, and sugar. Let sit overnight, stirring occasionally.

2. The next day, preheat oven to 350°F. Grease and flour a 12-cup bundt pan. Set aside.

3. In large bowl, combine peach mixture, cake mix, pudding, eggs, and oil. Beat for 3 minutes using an electric mixer set to high speed. Gently stir in pecans by hand.

4. Pour batter into the bundt pan and bake for 55 minutes.

5. Remove from oven and let cool completely.

6. Combine ¼ cup reserved peach liquid with 1⅓ cups confectioners' sugar to make a glaze. Drizzle glaze over cake.

# Amaretto Dream Cake

*This richly flavored layer cake combines the richness of cream cheese, the fruity sweetness of apricots, and the unmistakable flavor of amaretto.*

**INGREDIENTS | SERVES 8**

1 18.25-ounce box yellow cake mix

3 eggs

1 cup buttermilk

¼ cup plus 2 tablespoons amaretto, divided

¼ cup vegetable oil

1 15-ounce can apricot halves, drained

1 16-ounce box cream cheese

4 cups confectioners' sugar

1. Preheat oven to 350°F. Butter and flour two round 9" cake pans. Set aside.

2. Combine cake mix, eggs, buttermilk, ¼ cup amaretto, and oil. Beat for 4 minutes using an electric mixer set to low speed. Turn batter into cake pans.

3. Bake for 35 minutes. Allow cakes to cool completely.

4. When cakes are completely cool to the touch, lay cake layers on a clean, flat surface. Mark the middle of the cake layer with toothpicks. With toothpicks as your guide, slice horizontally, using a few slow even strokes of a serrated knife. Carefully remove top layer to a clean, flat surface. Repeat this process with the second layer to create four layers total.

5. Combine drained apricots and ½ cup plus two tablespoons amaretto in a blender and blend until completely smooth.

6. Center bottom layer of cake on platter. Smooth one third of the apricot mixture on top of the cake layer. Repeat for next two layers.

7. Beat cream cheese and remaining 3 tablespoons amaretto until cheese is soft. Add confectioners' sugar and beat until smooth. Frost cake with cream cheese mixture.

# Citrus Crush Cake

*This treat is perfect for summer parties and a sweet reminder of warmer days on a winter evening.*

**INGREDIENTS | SERVES 24**

1 18.25-ounce box yellow cake mix

3 eggs

1 can mandarin oranges

1 can crushed pineapple with juice

1 12-ounce tub nondairy whipped topping

1 3.9-ounce package instant vanilla pudding

1. Preheat oven to 350°F. Grease and flour 9" × 13" pan. Set aside.

2. Combine cake mix, eggs, and mandarin oranges using an electric mixer set to medium speed for 3 minutes. Turn batter into pan. Bake for 30 minutes. Allow to cool completely.

3. Combine crushed pineapple with juice, dessert topping, and vanilla pudding mix; stir to mix well. Top cooled cake with this mixture. Refrigerate until ready to serve.

# Shortcake Trifle

*Gather with friends and go to pick your own strawberries. Bring them home and enjoy each other's company while putting together this simple—and simply delicious— dessert. Or try this trifle with fruit salad instead of strawberry filling.*

**INGREDIENTS | SERVES 25**

2 18.25-ounce boxes angel food cake mix plus ingredients called for on boxes

2 16-ounce packages strawberry glaze

1 quart fresh strawberries, sliced

1 15-ounce tub nondairy whipped topping

1. Prepare and bake angel food cakes according to cake mix instructions. Cool cakes. Cut into cubes.

2. Combine sliced strawberries and glaze.

3. Place a layer of cake cubes in the bottom of a punch bowl. Top with a layer of strawberry mixture and then a layer of whipped topping. Repeat layers until bowl is full.

4. Top with a layer of whipped topping. Keep trifle cool until ready to serve.

# Cheesecake for 24

*Try this recipe with raspberry, blackberry, or blueberry pie filling. For a chocolaty twist, substitute chocolate cake mix for the white cake mix and chocolate whipped topping for the whipped topping. Garnish with chocolate syrup and chocolate shavings.*

**INGREDIENTS | SERVES 24**

1 18.25-ounce box white cake mix plus ingredients called for on box

4 cups confectioners' sugar

2 8-ounce boxes cream cheese, room temperature

1 15-ounce tub nondairy whipped topping

2 16-ounce cans cherry pie filling

1. Preheat oven to 350°F. Grease and flour two 9" x 13" cake pans. Set aside.

2. Prepare batter according to cake mix instructions. Divide batter evenly between cake pans. Bake for 20 minutes. Remove cakes from oven and allow to cool.

3. Meanwhile, use an electric mixer to beat together confectioners' sugar and cream cheese until fluffy. Fold whipped topping into cream cheese mixture.

4. Spread cream cheese mixture on cakes. Top with pie filling. Refrigerate until ready to serve.

# Pajama Party Pizza Cake

*To really impress your guests, serve this in a clean pizza box. (Ask your local pizzeria nicely; they'll probably give you one.) Use a pizza cutter to cut this into wedges and serve.*

## INGREDIENTS | SERVES 8

1 9-ounce box Jiffy golden brown cake mix plus ingredients called for on box

1 3-ounce package strawberry gelatin

1½ cups hot water

1 firm banana, sliced to resemble pepperoni

1 cup sliced strawberries

1 cup blueberries

Whipped topping

1. Preheat oven to 350°F. Grease and butter a pizza pan. Be sure to use a pan with a raised lip or batter will run over the edge.

2. Prepare cake batter according to package directions. Pour into pan and bake for 10 minutes.

3. Mix gelatin with water and let thicken.

4. Remove cake from oven and let cool. Arrange fruit on cake as you would pizza toppings. Pour thickened gelatin over all and chill.

5. Top with whipped topping and serve.

# Grown-Up Chocolate Trifle

*This dessert is best after being allowed to "set" for a day. The rich trifle makes a lovely presentation and is so easy to make!*

**INGREDIENTS** | **SERVES 8–10**

1 18.25-ounce box devil's food cake mix plus ingredients called for on box

2 3.9-ounce boxes instant chocolate pudding plus ingredients called for on boxes

2 15-ounce tubs whipped topping

Optional: ½ cup Kahlua

Maraschino cherries, strawberries, or raspberries for garnish

Chocolate syrup for garnish

1. Prepare and bake cake according to cake mix instructions for a 9" × 13" cake. Allow cake to cool completely.

2. Prepare both boxes of pudding according to package instructions.

3. Cut cake into quarters. Crumble one of the quarters into a large bowl. Layer 2 cups pudding on top of crumbled cake. Crumble another cake quarter and top with half a tub of whipped topping. Repeat for remaining cake quarters.

4. Douse generously with Kahlua if desired. Top with a dollop of whipped topping and garnish with cherries, strawberries, or raspberries. Drizzle with chocolate syrup.

5. Refrigerate overnight. Keep chilled until ready to serve.

# Lower-Cholesterol Apple Bake

*Here's a healthier take on a baked dessert. Bake this treat ahead of time and warm it up before serving. Garnish with whipped cream or ice cream for a cool, creamy contrast.*

**INGREDIENTS | SERVES 16**

1 18.25-ounce box yellow cake mix

½ cup low-cholesterol margarine, softened

¼ cup packed brown sugar

1 teaspoon ground cinnamon

2 large baking apples, cored, peeled, and thinly sliced

¼ cup cholesterol-free egg product (i.e., Egg Beaters)

1 cup low-fat sour cream

1. Preheat oven to 350°F. Grease baking pan.

2. Mix cake mix, margarine, brown sugar, and cinnamon until large crumbs form.

3. Set aside ⅔ cup of the crumb mixture. Press remaining mixture into the bottom of a rectangular baking pan. Arrange apples on top of this layer.

4. Combine egg product and sour cream and pour this mixture on top of the fruit. Top with reserved crumb mixture. Bake for 30 minutes or until topping browns slightly.

5. Cool before serving.

# Kahlua Cake

*Drizzle liquor on the grownups' cake and chocolate syrup on the kids'.*
*This elegant cake is lovely for parties and easy to transport.*

**INGREDIENTS | SERVES 8**

1 18.25-ounce box devil's food cake mix

1 3.9-ounce package instant chocolate pudding

1 pint sour cream

⅔ cup vegetable oil

4 eggs

2 cups semisweet chocolate chips

1 15-ounce tub nondairy whipped topping

1. Preheat to 350°F. Butter a 12-cup bundt pan. Set aside.

2. Thoroughly mix all ingredients except chocolate chips and whipped topping in a large bowl. Fold in chocolate chips. Pour mixture into the pan. Bake for 1 hour.

3. Cover and let cool in pan overnight. The next morning, flip pan over, cover again, and let set one more day. When ready to serve, garnish with whipped topping and drizzle with Kahlua.

# Family-Friendly Punch Bowl Trifle

*Easy to bake, easy to make, and lovely to see, this dish is a variation on a favorite recipe that's as delightful for the kids as it is for the adults.*

**INGREDIENTS | SERVES 25**

2 18.25-ounce boxes chocolate cake mix plus ingredients called for on boxes

2 12-ounce tubs chocolate whipped topping

1 20-ounce can cherry pie filling

1 15-ounce tub nondairy whipped topping

1. Prepare and bake cakes according to cake mix instructions. Cool cakes. Cut into cubes.

2. Place a layer of cake cubes in the bottom of a punch bowl. Add a layer of chocolate whipped topping. Add a layer of cherry pie filling. Repeat layers until bowl is full.

3. Top with plain whipped topping. Keep trifle cool until ready to serve.

# CHAPTER 8

# Cooking with Kids

# Toy Oven Cake

*While most adults can't imagine trying to bake a cake using a light bulb as a heat source, children have met this culinary challenge for years and years. Please note that small children should not cook unsupervised.*

**INGREDIENTS | SERVES 1 CHILD**

3 tablespoons cake mix
1 tablespoon milk
Frosting

1. Preheat toy oven as instructed by manufacturer. Grease and flour toy pan. Set aside.

2. Combine cake mix and milk. Beat with a fork until batter is smooth. Bake for about 15 minutes or until a toothpick comes out clean.

3. Allow cake to cool before frosting.

# Yummiest Play Dough Ever

*Finally, you don't have to stop the kids from eating the play dough. This recipe is not only fun, it's edible.*

**INGREDIENTS | SERVES 10 CHILDREN**

1 18.25-ounce box white cake mix
½ cup margarine, softened
3 tablespoons water
Food coloring

1. Mix cake mix and margarine in a large bowl. Add water bit by bit until dough reaches the desired consistency. Divide dough into batches and color each batch.

2. Store uneaten dough in plastic bags for future use.

## Little Helping Hands

Allow kids to choose food coloring and mix it into the dough themselves. You might want to do the initial mixing yourself because food coloring stains. Keep this in mind and have the kids wear old clothes or smocks. Kids will get a kick out of kneading the dough until it is mixed completely.

# Kisses from Kids Cupcakes

*This is a fun collaboration. Kids love the responsibility of placing the candies—even if they do eat a few.*

**INGREDIENTS | SERVES 12**

1 18.25-ounce box cake mix plus
   ingredients called for on box
12 chocolate kiss candies
Frosting

## Teachable Moments

Even young children can learn some basics of cooking. There's no better time to teach them than when you're doing a fun project together. They also love having a "job," so try to pick a step for young children to complete themselves when you're cooking.

1. Preheat oven according to cake mix instructions. Line a muffin tin with paper baking cups.

2. Prepare batter according to cake mix instructions for cupcakes. Fill baking cups with batter.

3. Allow kids to unwrap candies and place one candy in the middle of each cup of batter. It will sink on its own with a gentle tap.

4. Bake according to instructions on package. Allow cupcakes to cool completely before frosting.

# Heart-Shaped Cupcakes

*Want an easy way to show you care? These cupcakes are perfect for showers, parties, and Valentine's Day. If you don't have marbles, use aluminum foil rolled into marble-sized balls.*

**INGREDIENTS | SERVES 24**

Glass marbles
1 18.25-ounce box cake mix plus
   ingredients called for on box
1 16-ounce tub red or pink frosting

1. Preheat oven according to cake mix instructions. Line a muffin tin with paper baking cups. Place one marble on the outside of each cupcake cup so that a dent is formed, creating a heart-shaped baking cup.

2. Mix batter according to instructions. Pour batter into baking cups. As cakes rise, they will form heart-shaped tops.

3. Allow cakes to cool completely before frosting.

# Cake of Many Colors

*This is one of the most delicious art projects you can take on with children. Try not to go in with a preconceived notion of the looks of your product. You'll have more fun if you're in it for pure enjoyment.*

**INGREDIENTS | SERVES 8**

1 18.25-ounce box white cake mix plus ingredients called for on box
Food coloring
Frosting

1. Preheat oven according to cake mix instructions. Grease cake pan and set aside.

2. Prepare batter according to instructions. Spoon batter evenly into four bowls and add a few drops of food coloring to each bowl.

3. Allow children to mix coloring into the batter and then spoon batter into cake pan in any color order they like. Bake according to instructions.

4. Allow cake to cool completely before frosting.

# Fortune Cupcakes

*More than a clever and sweet dessert, this is a fun game for slightly older kids. Whether they help in the baking, the eating, or both, there's plenty to entertain in this project.*

**INGREDIENTS | SERVES 24**

1 18.25-ounce box cake mix plus ingredients called for on box
24 large gumdrops
2 16-ounce tubs prepared frosting

1. Preheat oven according to package instructions. Line a muffin tin with paper baking cups.

2. Prepare cake mix according to instructions. Place 1 gumdrop in each cupcake. Bake cupcakes. Allow cakes to cool completely before frosting.

3. Draw up a chart with different fortunes for each color of gumdrop. Eat the cupcakes to discover your fortune!

# No Bake Candy Treats

*These treats are easy to make and don't require an oven. Be warned:*
*You might eat a few while you make them.*

**INGREDIENTS | SERVES 24**

1 18.25-ounce box cake mix
1 16-ounce tub prepared frosting

Combine cake mix and frosting in a large mixing bowl. Mix thoroughly. Pinch off small amounts and roll into balls. Keep cool until ready to snack.

## No-Bake Snow People

For a wintry twist, use white cake mix and sour cream frosting to make the No Bake Candy Treats. Make snowmen out of the balls of dough and use sprinkles and other decorations to make faces. This project has very few steps but has fun sensory components. Talk your children through the steps and let them create their own snow people.

# Easy Protein Cookies

*Tofu is a great source of protein, and this is an easy way to sneak a little into the kids' diet. These cookies are so easy to make that they'll quickly become a go-to favorite.*

**INGREDIENTS | SERVES 24**

1 18.25-ounce box cake mix
½ cup silken tofu
¼ cup olive oil
1 egg

1. Preheat oven to 350°F.

2. Mix all ingredients well in a large mixing bowl. Drop by spoonfuls onto a nonstick cookie sheet. Bake for 20 minutes.

3. Allow to cool and remove to wire rack.

# Campfire Cobbler

*This easy recipe requires only two ingredients plus a Dutch oven
and a campfire. It's a memory maker, that's for sure.*

**INGREDIENTS | SERVES 8**

1 15-ounce can cherry or peach pie
  filling
1 18.25-ounce box white cake mix

### Historical Baking

Bakers of yore did not bake with cake mix
or canned pie filling, but they did bake in
the embers of a fire. Talk to your kids about
what it would be like to cook this way every
day. Ask them to imagine how life might be
different. Let your imagination wander—
that's what campfires are for.

1. Pour pie filling into the bottom of a Dutch oven. Pour dry cake mix over pie filling. Cover Dutch oven and place in the coals of a fire.

2. Place some hot coals on the lid of the Dutch oven. Cook for 15 minutes.

# Orange Campfire Cakes

*The rounded shape you can achieve here is amazing. The oranges lend a delicate flavor to the cake.*

**INGREDIENTS | SERVES 12**

1 (18.25-ounce) box white cake mix plus
  ingredients called for on box
12 oranges
2 16-ounce tubs sour cream frosting

1. Prepare cake batter according to instructions. Cut the tops off the oranges and hollow out the insides.

2. Fill each orange ¾ full with cake batter and surround the orange completely with tin foil.

3. Place foil-wrapped oranges in the hot part of the fire and wait for about 20 minutes, turning once.

4. Remove from fire and allow to cool. Frost if desired.

# Microwave Cake

*This recipe is so quick and easy that older kids can make it for themselves as a warm, nourishing after-school snack. It doesn't need icing, but it is great with ice cream.*

**INGREDIENTS | SERVES 8**

1 18.25-ounce box cake mix

1 15-ounce can pie filling

3 eggs

## Baking in a Microwave

While microwaves have become a staple in American kitchens, they are still far from the most reliable friend when it comes to baking. Intensity and heat vary, as will the time it takes to bake this cake. This recipe may take a couple of attempts to perfect, but once you get it, you'll love it.

1. Grease a microwave-safe dish. Mix all ingredients together in a large mixing bowl, taking care to combine completely. Pour batter into dish and shake until level.

2. Cook cake in the microwave for 10–12 minutes on high. Remove cake from microwave and allow to set for 3 minutes.

# Cinnamon Toast Cake

*This treat is lovely with coffee. When older kids decide to bring the folks breakfast in bed, this is an easy, wholesome option.*

**INGREDIENTS | SERVES 6**

1 18.25-ounce box white cake mix plus ingredients called for on box

Cinnamon-sugar mixture

¼ cup butter

## Breakfast in Bed

There's something kids like about serving the folks breakfast in bed now and then. If your kids are old enough and have the kitchen skills to safely pull this off, plant the idea in their heads. With any luck you'll get a great breakfast in bed and some fun family memories out of the deal.

1. Grease a microwavable dish. Mix batter according to cake mix instructions. Pour into dish. Sprinkle liberally with cinnamon-sugar mixture.

2. Microwave on high for 10 minutes. Remove cake from microwave. Dot warm cake with butter and sprinkle again with cinnamon-sugar mixture.

3. Let cake stand 3 minutes before serving.

# Mardi Gras Cakes

*Traditional king cakes baked in New Orleans have a little plastic baby doll hidden inside. Whoever finds the baby gets good luck. We've avoided choking hazards here by substituting a gumdrop for a plastic toy.*

**INGREDIENTS** | **SERVES 24**

1 18.25-ounce box cake mix plus ingredients called for on box

1 16-ounce tub prepared frosting

Food coloring

Sprinkles and other decorations

1 gumdrop

1. Preheat oven according to cake mix instructions. Line a muffin tin with paper baking cups.

2. Prepare batter according to instructions for cupcakes. Pour into muffin cups. Allow your child to hide a candy in one of the cups of batter.

3. Bake according to instructions. Allow cupcakes to cool completely.

4. Separate the tub of frosting into smaller batches and color them with food coloring. Allow your child to stir the color into the frosting. Frost and decorate cupcakes.

5. Before serving, explain that the person who finds the candy in his or her cupcake can look forward to a year of good luck.

# Magic Potion Cookies

*Let the kids figure out what to add in. Let them try combinations and measure them out themselves. Nothing's more fun than a "magic potion" cooked up by mad scientists. Who knows? You might invent a favorite cookie.*

**INGREDIENTS | SERVES 24**

1 18.25-ounce box yellow cake mix

3 eggs

⅓ cup oil

½ teaspoon vanilla

1 cup oatmeal

3 cups add-ins: candies, chocolate morsels, coconut, nuts, trail mix, or other favorites

1. Preheat oven to 350°F.

2. Mix cake mix, eggs, oil, vanilla, and oatmeal together in a large mixing bowl. Let children choose, measure, and add their own combination of add-ins.

3. Drop cookies by spoonfuls onto an ungreased cookie sheet. Bake for 9 minutes. Remove from oven and cool on a wire rack.

## Imaginative Baking

Kids love to mix foods. While they might scream when the macaroni touches the green beans, they'll sometimes jump at the chance to brew concoctions. Let them get imaginative with the add-ins. They'll love the sense of involvement and the cookies they produce!

# Berry Snacky Pizza

*The surprisingly lovely flavors of sweet, fruity raspberry filling and sharp Cheddar cheese are inspiring.*

**INGREDIENTS | SERVES 6**

1 18.25-ounce box white cake mix
1 cup quick-cooking oats
½ cup grated Colby or Cheddar cheese
½ cup butter, softened
1 egg
1 21-ounce can raspberry pie filling

1. Preheat oven to 350°F. Grease a round, solid-bottomed pizza pan.

2. In a large mixing bowl, combine cake mix, oats, grated cheese, and ½ cup butter.

3. Mix thoroughly using an electric mixer set to low speed until a crumbly mixture forms. Remove 1 cup of mixture and place in a separate, smaller bowl.

4. Add egg to the remaining mixture and mix well. Press into the pizza pan. Bake for 10 minutes.

5. Remove baked crust from oven and layer on pie filling like pizza sauce. Top with reserved crumb mixture and additional grated cheese if desired.

6. Bake an additional 15 minutes. Allow pizza to cool somewhat before serving.

# Peanut Butter Cake

*Play to favorite—and familiar—flavors for the young, picky eaters in
your life. This nutty recipe is a winner with the small fry.*

### INGREDIENTS | SERVES 8

1 18.25-ounce box yellow cake mix
3 eggs, beaten
1⅓ cups water
½ cup crunchy peanut butter
Peanut Butter Icing (page 128)

1. Preheat oven to 350°F. Butter and flour a 9" × 13" cake pan.

2. In a large mixing bowl, combine cake mix, eggs, water, and peanut butter. Using an electric mixer set to medium speed, beat the mixture for 3 full minutes.

3. Turn batter into pan and bake for 35 minutes. Allow cake to cool completely before frosting.

### Add Layers

To make your PB cake an extra special PBJ cake, invert it onto a serving platter. Mark the center with toothpicks all the way around. Slice the cake in half horizontally and fill with a generous layer of your favorite jelly. Try this on cupcakes as well.

# Peanut Butter Icing

*Slightly reminiscent of the filling of a Buckeye or peanut butter cup,*
*this icing is so easy the kids can make it themselves.*

**INGREDIENTS | SERVES 8**

½ cup crunchy peanut butter
¼ cup butter, softened
6 tablespoons heavy cream
1 pound confectioners' sugar
Dash salt
1½ teaspoons vanilla

Use an electric mixer to cream peanut butter and butter. Slowly incorporate cream, sugar, salt, and vanilla. Use this mixture to frost cooled cake.

# Four-Ingredient Apple Bake

*If your kids are old enough to handle the oven, they can do this with minor supervision. If they're not*
*quite ready to touch the oven, you can do that part for them—but they can set the timer.*

**INGREDIENTS | SERVES 12**

1 18.25-ounce box spice cake mix
3 eggs
1 15-ounce can apple pie filling
1 16-ounce tub nondairy whipped
  topping

1. Preheat oven to 350°F.

2. Mix together cake mix, eggs, and apple pie filling. Pour into a 9" × 13" pan. Bake for 45 minutes. Remove from oven and allow to cool until just warm. Top with whipped topping.

# Choco-Cherry Cake

*Similar to the apple bake, this simple recipe is an easy and rewarding project for brand new cooks.*

**INGREDIENTS | SERVES 12**

1 18.25-ounce box chocolate cake mix
3 eggs
1 15-ounce can cherry pie filling
Vanilla ice cream
Chocolate syrup

1. Preheat oven to 350°F.

2. Combine cake mix, eggs, and pie filling in a large mixing bowl. Pour batter into a 9" × 13" baking dish. Bake for 45 minutes. Serve warm with a scoop of ice cream and a drizzle of syrup.

# Slow Cooker Cobbler

*A slow cooker is a great place for older kids to try cooking on their own. This easy and delicious dessert requires no lifting in and out of the oven. Adults will still want to supervise, but the kids can probably handle this all on their own.*

**INGREDIENTS | SERVES 8**

1 16-ounce can cherry pie filling
1⅓ cups chocolate cake mix
1 egg
3 tablespoons evaporated milk
Cocoa powder for dusting

1. Grease the inside of the slow cooker or Crock Pot with butter.

2. Pour pie filling into slow cooker and cook on high for 30 minutes. Combine remaining ingredients in a small mixing bowl. Spoon mixture on top of warm pie filling. Cover and cook for 2½ hours. Dust each serving lightly with cocoa powder.

# Mud Pie Cupcakes

*Decorations hold up better if the icing has a few minutes to set. To make sure gummy worms—and other decorations—stay in place, let icing rest for 10 minutes before serving.*

**INGREDIENTS | SERVES 24**

1 18.25-ounce box chocolate cake mix plus ingredients called for on box

1 16-ounce tub chocolate frosting

2 cups crumbled chocolate sandwich cookies

Chocolate syrup for garnish

1 8-ounce package gummy worms

1. Prepare and bake cupcakes according to cake mix instructions. Allow cupcakes to cool completely before frosting. Top frosting with cookie crumbles and drizzle with chocolate syrup.

2. Halve gummy worms. Place each cut edge in frosting to create the illusion of a worm slithering in mud.

# Ice Cream Sandwiches with Sprinkles

*Ice cream sandwiches are a summer favorite for kids of all ages. What could be better than baking up a batch of your very own? Wrap finished sandwiches in foil and store in the freezer where they'll be ready for playdates and after-school snacks.*

**INGREDIENTS** | **MAKES 24 SANDWICHES**

⅔ cup butter

2 eggs

1 18.25-ounce box devil's food cake

1 tub ice cream

Sprinkles or jimmies to taste

1. Preheat oven to 350°F.

2. Combine butter and egg. Stir in cake mix. Blend together well. Drop by spoonfuls onto a greased cookie sheet. Bake cookies for 10–12 minutes.

3. Remove cookies to cooling rack. When cookies are cool, invite kids to sandwich 2 tablespoons of ice cream between two cookies. Roll cookies through sprinkles or jimmies so they stick to the ice cream. Wrap in foil and freeze.

# CHAPTER 9

# Cake Mix Cookies

# Blank Canvas Cookie Recipe

*This is a very basic cookie recipe that's perfect if you're just itching to experiment. Add baking chips or dried fruit to your choice of cake mix for a flavor combination that's yours and yours alone.*

**INGREDIENTS | 4 DOZEN COOKIES**

1 18.25-ounce box cake mix (any flavor)
½ cup butter, softened
1 egg

1. Preheat oven to 350°F.

2. Combine cake mix, softened butter, egg, and any add-ins that strike your fancy. Mix using an electric mixer set to low speed.

3. Drop batter by spoonfuls onto ungreased cookie sheets, leaving two inches between cookies. Bake for 12 minutes or until golden.

4. Let cookies cool on the pan for 3 minutes. Gently remove to a serving plate.

# German Chocolate Cake Cookies

*This lighter-tasting chocolate cookie provides that little taste of chocolate you're looking for without the heavy sugar or high caffeine.*

**INGREDIENTS | 4 DOZEN COOKIES**

1 18.25-ounce box German chocolate cake mix
1 cup semisweet chocolate chips
1 cup oatmeal
½ cup vegetable oil
2 eggs, slightly beaten
½ cup raisins
1 teaspoon vanilla

1. Preheat oven to 350°F.

2. Combine all ingredients. Mix well using electric mixer set to low speed. If floury crumbs develop, add a dribble of water.

3. Drop dough by spoonfuls onto an ungreased cookie sheet. Bake for 10 minutes. Cool completely before lifting cookies off sheet and onto a serving dish.

# Oatmeal and Chocolate Chip Cookies

*Oatmeal is a great source of vitamins, minerals, and fiber. It is also reputed to be a natural antidepressant. These cookies are a great way to sneak some oatmeal into your diet.*

**INGREDIENTS** | **MAKES 24 COOKIES**

1 18-ounce box yellow cake mix
⅔ cup rolled oats
½ cup margarine
1 egg
½ cup chocolate chips

1. Preheat oven to 375°F.

2. Combine cake mix, oats, margarine, and egg in a bowl and mix well. Fold in chocolate chips. Drop by spoonfuls onto an ungreased cookie sheet.

3. Bake for 10 minutes, or until lightly golden. Remove warm cookies from sheet and allow to cool on a wire rack.

# Peanut Butter Cup Cookies

*Peanut butter and chocolate complement each other as few other foods do. Enjoy this decadent treat with a glass of cold chocolate milk.*

**INGREDIENTS** | **MAKES 24 COOKIES**

1 18.25-ounce box chocolate cake mix
½ cup butter, softened
2 eggs
½ cup semisweet chocolate morsels
½ cup peanut butter morsels

1. Preheat oven to 350°F.

2. Mix cake mix, butter, and eggs together in a bowl to form a smooth batter. Fold in chocolate and peanut butter morsels. Drop by spoonfuls onto an ungreased cookie sheet.

3. Bake for 9 minutes. Remove from oven and allow cookies to set for 5 minutes before removing them to a wire rack. Allow cookies to cool completely.

# Double-Devil Chocolate Crunch Cookies

*The devil himself would find this recipe heavenly. The rich chocolate taste and satisfying coconut are a winning combination. Just be sure to avoid cake mixes with pudding for this recipe.*

**INGREDIENTS | MAKES 60 COOKIES**

1 18.25-ounce box devil's food cake mix

½ cup vegetable oil

2 eggs, slightly beaten

½ cup chopped pecans

5 regular milk chocolate bars, divided into squares

½ cup sweetened flaked coconut

1. Preheat oven to 350°F.

2. Combine devil's food cake mix, vegetable oil, and eggs in a bowl and mix completely. Gently fold pecans into batter.

3. Drop batter by spoonfuls onto ungreased cookie sheets. Bake for 10 minutes. Remove when cookies are set but still a bit soft in the center.

4. Place one square of milk chocolate on each cookie. When it melts, spread to create a chocolate coating on the cookie's top.

5. Transfer cookies immediately to a wire rack and allow them to cool completely.

# Chocolate Biscotti

*This is an elegant treat with a good cup of coffee and friendly conversation.*
*You can make them far in advance; biscotti keep for weeks.*

**INGREDIENTS | MAKES 36 BISCOTTI**

1 18-ounce box chocolate cake mix
1 cup all-purpose flour
½ cup melted butter
¼ cup chocolate syrup
2 eggs
1 teaspoon vanilla extract
1 12-ounce package miniature semisweet
  chocolate chips

1. Preheat oven to 350°F.

2. Mix dry cake mix, flour, butter, chocolate syrup, eggs, and vanilla well in a large bowl. Fold in chocolate chips.

3. Divide the batter in half. Shape each half into a 12" × 2" log. Place both halves on an ungreased baking sheet. Bake for 30 minutes.

4. Remove from oven and let cool for 15 minutes. Transfer logs to a cutting board and carefully cut into ½" slices. Cutting on the diagonal is easiest.

5. Return slices to the baking sheet and bake for another 15 minutes. Remove from oven and cool biscotti on wire racks.

# Coconut Kisses

*Rich, sweet coconut and irresistible dark chocolate meld together
beautifully in this luscious, decadent cookie.*

**INGREDIENTS | MAKES 24 COOKIES**

1 18-ounce box white cake mix
½ cup vegetable oil
2 eggs, slightly beaten
1 cup dark chocolate chips
1 cup shredded sweetened coconut

1. Preheat oven to 350°F. Lightly grease a cookie sheet. Set aside.

2. Mix cake mix, vegetable oil, and eggs in a bowl to form a smooth batter. Fold in chocolate chips. Fold in coconut.

3. Use a tablespoon to drop balls of cookie dough onto the cookie sheet. Bake for 10 minutes or until golden.

4. Remove cookies from oven and allow to cool on a wire rack.

# Butter-Pecan Cookies

*These are a quick fix when you want a rich, buttery treat. Serve with pralines, caramel, and/or
creamy vanilla ice cream for an interesting take on the ice cream sundae.*

**INGREDIENTS | MAKES 24 COOKIES**

1 18.25-ounce box butter pecan cake mix
2 eggs, slightly beaten
½ cup vegetable oil
2 tablespoons water

1. Preheat oven to 350°F.

2. Combine ingredients and mix to form an even batter. Drop by spoonfuls onto an ungreased cookie sheet. Bake for 15 minutes or until golden and set.

3. Let cool on cookie sheet for 5 minutes. Remove to wire rack to cool completely.

# Peanut Butter Cookies

*This lunchbox classic is a favorite with the whole family, and this recipe is a cinch to whip up.*

**INGREDIENTS** | **MAKES 24 COOKIES**

1 18-ounce box yellow cake mix
1 cup peanut butter
½ cup vegetable oil
2 tablespoons water
2 large eggs

1. Preheat oven to 350°F.

2. Combine all ingredients and mix thoroughly. Use a teaspoon to drop balls of cookie dough onto an ungreased cookie sheet.

3. Laying the tines of a fork across the top of each cookie, press down to create a crisscross pattern. Bake for 12 minutes. Allow cookies to cool for 2 minutes on the warm cookie sheet.

4. Remove cookies to a wire rack and let cool completely.

# Peanut Butter Kisses

*These wholesome cookies are so easy to bake you can have them quickly at the ready for any occasion.*

**INGREDIENTS** | **MAKES 24 COOKIES**

1 18.25-ounce box yellow cake mix
2 eggs
½ cup vegetable oil
1 cup crunchy peanut butter
2 teaspoons water

1. Preheat oven to 350°F.

2. Combine all ingredients in a large mixing bowl. Use an electric mixer to blend completely.

3. Drop dough by spoonfuls onto nonstick cookie sheet, leaving 2 inches between cookies. Laying the tines of a fork across the top of each cookie, press down to create a crisscross pattern.

4. Bake cookies for 12 minutes. Remove cookies to a wire rack to cool completely.

# Whipped Cream Brownie Bakers

*Who can resist the sweetness of whipped topping? This cookie pairs whipped topping and rich chocolate for a taste that's sure to satisfy.*

**INGREDIENTS | MAKES 48 COOKIES**

1 18-ounce box chocolate cake mix
1 tablespoon cocoa powder
1 egg
1 cup pecans, chopped
¼ cup confectioners' sugar
4 ounces whipped topping

1. Preheat oven to 350°F.

2. Combine cake mix, cocoa powder, and egg and mix well. Gently fold pecans into dough.

3. Sift confectioners' sugar into a separate bowl. Coat your hands with confectioners' sugar, then shape dough into small balls. Coat cookie balls with confectioners' sugar.

4. Place onto cookie sheet, leaving 2 inches between cookies. Bake 12 minutes or until set. Remove from oven and transfer to wire rack to cool. Top with whipped topping.

# Double Chocolate Chip Cookies

*Chocolate chip cookies are delicious, so make someone's day with a dark, decadent delight.*

**INGREDIENTS | MAKES 36 COOKIES**

1 18-ounce box devil's food cake mix
   with pudding
½ cup water
2 eggs
1 cup semisweet chocolate morsels

1. Preheat oven to 375°F. Grease cookie sheet. Set aside.

2. Mix all ingredients in a bowl using electric mixer on low speed.

3. When batter is completely smooth, drop by spoonfuls onto the cookie sheet, leaving 2 inches between cookies. Bake for 9 minutes.

4. Remove from oven and allow cookies to cool for 1 minute before removing them to a wire rack to cool completely.

# Harvest Cookies

*This autumnal treat is lovely with a cup of hot cider. Cranberry raisins give these cookies a zippy, tangy taste that's a perfect complement to a glass of cold milk.*

**INGREDIENTS** | **MAKES 60 COOKIES**

1 18-ounce box spice cake mix
1 cup cranberry raisins
½ cup vegetable oil
½ cup applesauce
1 egg

1. Preheat oven to 350°F.

2. Combine all ingredients in a large bowl. Mix for 1 minute with an electric mixer set to medium speed.

3. Drop batter by spoonful onto an ungreased cookie sheet, leaving 2 inches between cookies. Bake for 12 minutes.

4. Let cool on cookie sheet before removing to a serving dish.

# Lemon-Lover's Cookies

*There's nothing so refreshing and elegant as a lemon cookie. These cookies are equally good as a summer treat or a winter refreshment.*

**INGREDIENTS** | **MAKES 36 BARS**

1 18-ounce box lemon cake mix
1 egg, slightly beaten
1 cup confectioners' sugar
1 8-ounce tub whipped topping
1 tablespoon lemon juice
1 cup confectioners' sugar
Lemon zest to taste

1. Preheat oven to 350°F. Lightly grease a cookie sheet and set aside.

2. Gently mix all ingredients except lemon zest. Drop by teaspoon into confectioners' sugar and roll to coat. Place on a cookie sheet.

3. Bake for 10 minutes, watching carefully to make sure cookies do not overbake. Remove from oven. Sprinkle with lemon zest. Let cool on cookie sheet.

# Sandwich Cookies

*Remember the sandwich cookies that were served during snack-time at school? The home-baked version is even better!*

**INGREDIENTS | MAKES 12 COOKIES**

1 18.25-ounce box devil's food cake mix
2 eggs
2 tablespoons water
2 tablespoons oil
½ cup cocoa powder
1 0.25-ounce envelope unflavored gelatin
¼ cup cold water
1 cup shortening
1 teaspoon vanilla
1 pound plus 1 cup confectioners' sugar

1. Preheat oven to 400°F. Grease a cookie sheet.

2. Combine cake mix, eggs, water, oil, and cocoa powder. Mix well using electric mixer on medium speed.

3. Butter your hands, form dough into balls, and place on the cookie sheet. Flatten each ball with the palm of your hand or a fork. Bake for 9 minutes.

4. Remove cookies to a paper towel. Flatten each cookie with the bottom of a clean mug. Let cool for 20 minutes.

5. In a smaller, microwave-safe bowl, mix gelatin powder and cold water. Heat in microwave until gelatin is transparent. Set gelatin mixture aside to cool completely.

6. Meanwhile, in a separate bowl beat the shortening until fluffy. Gently fold in vanilla and confectioners' sugar. Mix cooled gelatin into shortening mixture.

7. Sandwich the filling between two cookies, rounded sides facing out. Serve with milk for dunking.

# Lemon Squares

*Colorful and flavorful with a creamy melt-in-your-mouth texture, this quick-bake take on a time-tested Southern favorite is sure to please.*

**INGREDIENTS | MAKES 24 SQUARES**

1 18-ounce box lemon cake mix
4 eggs, divided use
¾ cup melted butter, divided use
¾ cup buttermilk
⅓ cup freshly squeezed lemon juice
⅓ cup sugar
1 tablespoon grated lemon zest
3 tablespoons confectioners' sugar
Paper-thin lemon slices to garnish

1. Preheat oven to 350°F.

2. Line a 9" × 13" Pyrex pan with aluminum foil. Leave enough foil sticking up from the pan to allow you to use it to lift out the baked bars. Grease the foil.

3. Set aside 1 cup cake mix; reserve for later use.

4. In a large mixing bowl, beat the remaining cake mix, 1 egg, and ¼ cup melted butter with an electric mixer on low speed to form a smooth batter.

5. Pat this mixture into the bottom of the pan.

6. In a separate bowl, mix remaining 3 eggs, remaining ½ cup melted butter, buttermilk, lemon juice, sugar, and lemon zest. Beat for 2 minutes with an electric mixer on medium speed.

7. Add lemon mixture over batter layer in pan. Bake for 35 minutes or until set and golden.

8. Use oven mitts to lift cookies out of pan by the aluminum foil edges. Remove to wire rack to cool completely. Sprinkle with confectioners' sugar and garnish with lemon slices.

# Chocolate and Strawberry Cookies

*These pink and brown cookies make a lovely presentation. They bring to mind the lusciousness of a chocolate-covered strawberry.*

**INGREDIENTS | MAKES 24 COOKIES**

1 18-ounce box strawberry cake mix
½ cup softened butter
2 eggs
1 cup dark chocolate chips

1. Preheat oven to 350°F.

2. Mix cake mix, butter, and eggs until very well blended. Fold in chocolate chips. Drop dough by spoonfuls onto an ungreased cookie sheet. Bake for 9 minutes.

3. Cool cookies on baking sheet for 3 minutes before removing to a cooling rack.

# Angel Food Cookies

*Serve these light and tasty morsels with dark coffee and ripe strawberries and you'll have a treat to remember.*

**INGREDIENTS | MAKES 24 COOKIES**

1 16-ounce box one-step angel food cake mix
½ cup diet lemon-lime soft drink
1 teaspoon vanilla extract

1. Preheat oven to 350°F. Grease cookie sheet and set aside.

2. Mix all ingredients together. Drop cookies by spoonfuls onto the cookie sheet. Bake for 5 minutes, watching closely. Remove before cookies turn brown.

3. Remove to wax paper and allow to cool completely.

# Best-Ever Brownies

*Don't let the lighter taste of German chocolate cake fool you. These brownies are rich and delicious by anyone's standards.*

**INGREDIENTS** | **MAKES 20 BROWNIES**

1 18.25-ounce box German chocolate cake mix
1 cup chopped walnuts
⅓ cup plus ½ cup evaporated milk
½ cup melted butter
1 14-ounce package vanilla caramels
1 cup dark chocolate chips

1. Preheat oven to 350°F.

2. Combine cake mix, nuts, ⅓ cup evaporated milk, and butter in a large bowl and mix well. Layer half of the batter into a 13" × 9" × 2" Pyrex dish.

3. Bake for 8 minutes. Remove from oven.

4. Melt together caramels and remaining ½ cup evaporated milk in the top of a double boiler. Pour mixture over baked layer.

5. Layer chocolate chips on top of caramel/milk mixture. Press remaining batter on top of the chocolate chip layer. Return to oven and bake for 30 minutes.

6. Remove from oven and let cool completely in pan.

# Lemon Mint Cookies

*Lemon and mint is a refreshing flavor combination that's quite sophisticated. The ground chocolate chips and cream cheese make the cookies creamy, and the tart, minty frosting is a wonderful flavor contrast.*

**INGREDIENTS | YIELDS 32 COOKIES**

1 18.25-ounce package lemon cake mix

²/₃ cup white chocolate chips, ground

2 eggs

⅓ cup melted butter

1 3-ounce package cream cheese, softened

¼ cup butter, softened

3 cups powdered sugar

⅓ cup lemon juice

½ teaspoon mint extract

1. Preheat oven to 325°F. Line 2 cookie sheets with parchment paper and set aside.

2. In large bowl, combine cake mix, ground white chocolate, eggs, and butter and mix well until combined. Batter is very thick; you may need to use your hands.

3. Form into 1" balls and place on prepared cookie sheets. Flatten slightly with your palm. Bake for 7–11 minutes or until the cookies are puffed and just set. Slide the parchment paper onto a cooling rack; let cool, then peel cookies off paper.

4. In medium bowl, combine cream cheese and butter; beat until smooth. Alternately beat in the powdered sugar and lemon juice until desired consistency is reached. Beat in mint extract. Frost cookies and let stand until set.

# Peanut Butter Tea Cakes

*Like a Russian Tea Cake, but flavored with peanut butter and made
easy with a cake mix, these cookies are so good!*

INGREDIENTS | YIELDS 48 COOKIES

½ cup butter, softened
¾ cup peanut butter
1 18.25-ounce package yellow cake mix
4 dozen chocolate kisses, unwrapped
Powdered sugar

## Chilling Dough

Chilling dough makes a more tender cookie. The gluten in the flour has a chance to relax a bit, which makes the dough easier to handle. Chilling also makes soft doughs a bit harder, so the insides stay soft and tender while the outside becomes crisp.

1. In large bowl, combine butter and peanut butter and mix well. Add yellow cake mix; mix until a dough forms. Cover and chill for 4–6 hours.

2. When ready to bake, preheat oven to 400°F. Roll dough by tablespoons around a chocolate Kiss; form into a ball and place on parchment paper–lined cookie sheet.

3. Bake cookies for 8–12 minutes or until just set. Let cool on sheet for 3 minutes, then drop into powdered sugar and roll to coat. Let cool completely on wire racks, then coat in powdered sugar again when cool.

# Richest Yellow Cake Cookies

*These surprisingly rich cookies are great with frosting but still fantastic on their own.*
*They're so easy to bake that you'll want to try them all kinds of ways.*

### INGREDIENTS | MAKES 24 COOKIES

¼ cup butter, softened

1 8-ounce package cream cheese, softened

1 egg yolk

¼ teaspoon vanilla extract

1 18-ounce box yellow cake mix

1. Preheat oven to 375°F.

2. Cream butter and cream cheese. Mix in egg yolk and vanilla. Add dry cake mix a little at a time, mixing well as you go. Cover and refrigerate for 2 hours.

3. Drop rounded spoonfuls onto an ungreased baking sheet. Bake for 12 minutes or until lightly golden.

# Granola White Chocolate Cookies

*These tender and chewy cookies are perfect for the lunchbox or a coffee break.*

### INGREDIENTS | YIELDS 36 COOKIES

1 18.25-ounce package yellow cake mix

¾ cup butter, softened

½ cup packed brown sugar

2 eggs

1 cup granola

1 cup white chocolate chips

1 cup dried cherries

1. Preheat oven to 375°F. In large bowl, combine cake mix, butter, brown sugar, and eggs and beat until batter forms.

2. Stir in granola and white chocolate chips. Drop by teaspoonfuls about 2 inches apart on ungreased cookie sheets.

3. Bake for 10–12 minutes or until cookies are light golden brown around the edges. Cool on cookie sheets for 3 minutes, then remove to wire rack to remove completely.

# Old Fashioned Sugar Cookies

*Sugar cookies have a flaky texture that is achieved by cutting the butter into the cake mix.*

**INGREDIENTS | YIELDS 48 COOKIES**

1 18.25-ounce white cake mix
¾ cup butter
2 egg whites
2 tablespoons light cream

### Easy Variations

Use different flavors of cake mix to make different types of sugar cookies, but use the butter, egg whites, and cream for a flaky texture. These can be frosted or glazed, or sprinkle them with colored sugar before baking for a festive touch.

1. Place cake mix in large bowl. Using a pastry blender or two forks, cut in butter until particles are fine. Blend in egg whites and cream until mixed. Shape dough into a ball and cover.

2. Chill for at least two hours and as many as 8 hours in refrigerator. Then preheat oven to 375°F. Roll dough into 1" balls and place on ungreased cookie sheets. Flatten to ¼" thickness with bottom of glass.

3. Bake for 7–10 minutes or until cookie edges are light brown. Cool on cookie sheets for 2 minutes, then remove to wire racks to cool completely. Serve as is or frost as desired.

# CHAPTER 10

# Cupcakes

# Coconut Cupcakes

*Coconut cake is a favorite pick at parties and daytime events. This rich, sweet cupcake is a sophisticated treat. Garnish with jellybeans for an easy springtime treat.*

**INGREDIENTS | MAKES 24 CUPCAKES**

1 18.25-ounce box white cake mix with pudding
1¼ cups buttermilk
2 eggs
¼ cup softened butter
2 teaspoons vanilla extract
½ teaspoon coconut extract
1 recipe Whipping Cream (page 166)
Semisweet chocolate chips for garnish
Sweetened flaked coconut for garnish

1. Preheat oven to 350°F. Line a muffin tin with paper baking cups. Spray lightly with cooking spray.

2. Using an electric mixer set on low speed, combine the cake mix, buttermilk, eggs, butter, and extracts until a moist batter begins to form.

3. Turn batter into cups, filling just a touch more than half full. Bake for 25 minutes. Allow cupcakes to cool completely.

4. Frost cupcakes with Whipping Cream and garnish with flaked coconut and a few chocolate chips.

# Chocolate Cupcakes

*The chocolate cupcake is the little black dress of the dessert world. Consider topping these cupcakes with whipped cream and chocolate shavings. You'll need to refrigerate them and serve shortly after frosting, but nothing beats the taste.*

**INGREDIENTS | SERVES 36**

1 18.25-ounce box chocolate or devil's food cake mix
1 teaspoon baking powder
1½ cups water
1 egg

1. Preheat oven to 350°F. Line a muffin tin with paper baking cups.

2. Combine all ingredients in a large bowl, using an electric mixer to beat until a smooth batter forms. Turn batter into baking cups, filling each paper cup ½ full.

3. Bake according to cake mix instructions. Frost with whipped topping or prepared frosting.

# Peanut Butter Cupcakes

*For chocolate/peanut butter frosting, combine 1 16-ounce tub dark chocolate frosting and ⅓ cup chunky natural peanut butter. It's an easy frosting that's sure to get rave reviews.*

**INGREDIENTS | MAKES 24 CUPCAKES**

1 18.25-ounce box yellow cake mix plus ingredients called for on box

½ cup natural, chunky peanut butter

1. Preheat oven to 350°F. Line a muffin tin with paper baking cups.

2. Prepare cake mix according to instructions. Add peanut butter just after you add the eggs.

3. Spoon batter into baking cups, filling each more than half full. Bake for 20 minutes. Allow cupcakes to cool on a rack.

# Gooey Praline Cupcakes

*The candied sweetness of the praline has been a traditional favorite for hundreds of years. Now you can get the taste—and the crunch—with much less work.*

**INGREDIENTS | MAKES 24 CUPCAKES**

1 18.25-ounce box yellow cake mix

1 cup buttermilk

¼ cup vegetable oil

4 eggs

Caramel ice cream topping

Chopped pecans for garnish

72 pralines

1. Preheat oven to 350°F. Line a muffin tin with paper baking cups.

2. Combine cake mix, buttermilk, oil, and eggs in a large mixing bowl and beat using an electric mixer set to low speed until a smooth batter forms. Fill baking cups halfway.

3. Bake 15 minutes or until tops are golden. Remove cupcakes from the oven and allow to cool completely before adding toppings.

4. Top cupcakes with caramel topping; sprinkle with pecans and garnish with 3 pralines per cupcake.

# Piña Colada Cupcakes

*This light, tropical blend of flavors is a favorite for summer parties or beach-themed affairs. To toast coconut, spread sweetened flaked coconut in a baking dish and bake at 350°F for 15 minutes, stirring frequently. You can do this while the cupcakes are cooling.*

**INGREDIENTS | MAKES 24 CUPCAKES**

1 18.25-ounce box white cake mix

1 3.9-ounce box instant French vanilla pudding mix

¼ cup vegetable oil

½ cup water

⅔ cup light rum, divided

4 eggs

1 14-ounce can plus 1 cup crushed pineapple

1 cup sweetened, flaked coconut

1 16-ounce tub vanilla frosting

1 12-ounce tub nondairy whipped topping

Toasted coconut for garnish

Cocktail parasols

1. Preheat oven to 350°F. Butter and flour two 8" layer cake pans.

2. Mix cake mix, pudding mix, oil, water, and ⅓ cup rum using an electric mixer on medium speed. Add eggs one at a time, slowly beating the batter as you go.

3. Fold in can of pineapple and coconut. Pour into pans and bake for 25 minutes.

4. To make the frosting, mix 1 cup crushed pineapple, remaining ⅓ cup rum, and vanilla frosting until thick. Add nondairy whipped topping.

5. Frost completely cooled cupcakes and garnish with toasted coconut and a parasol.

# Chocolate Truffle Cupcakes

*This is a perfectly delightful treasure for the true chocolate lover.*
*These rich cupcakes have a surprisingly creamy, molten center.*

**INGREDIENTS | SERVES 24**

1 cup semisweet chocolate chips
½ cup butter
3 eggs
3 egg yolks
1 16-ounce package brownie mix
2 tablespoons chocolate milk
2 tablespoons confectioners' sugar
¼ cup cocoa powder

1. Preheat oven to 400°F. Line a muffin tin with paper baking cups.

2. In a microwave-safe bowl, combine chocolate chips and butter.

3. Microwave on high for 60 seconds, stirring halfway through. Set aside to cool for at least 5 minutes.

4. In a larger mixing bowl, combine eggs and yolks; use an electric mixer to beat on high speed for 5 minutes. The eggs should look foamy and double in volume.

5. Fold dry brownie mix, chocolate milk, and microwaved chocolate mixture into the egg mixture using a wooden spoon. Pour even amounts into the baking cups.

6. Bake for 13 minutes. The centers of the cake should be soft, but the edges should be set. Sprinkle cupcakes with confectioners' sugar and cocoa powder.

# Perfect Lemon Cupcakes

*We associate lemon smells and flavors with light, clean, happy experiences. These cupcakes make the most of that association by offering a sunny burst of flavors.*

**INGREDIENTS | MAKES 24 CUPCAKES**

1 18.25-ounce box lemon cake mix
1 cup buttermilk
¼ cup vegetable oil
4 eggs
1 12-ounce tub ready-to-spread frosting

1. Preheat oven to 350°F. Line a muffin tin with paper baking cups.

2. Combine all ingredients in a large mixing bowl and beat using an electric mixer set to low speed until a smooth batter forms. Turn batter into cups, filling halfway.

3. Bake 15 minutes or until tops are golden. Remove cupcakes from the oven and allow to cool completely before frosting.

# Chocolate Chip Cupcakes

*Warm chocolate chips are the ultimate comfort food. Match that sensual flavor with moist buttermilk cake for a home-baked sensation. Choose chocolate chips with a higher cocoa content for a richer taste.*

**INGREDIENTS | SERVES 24**

1 18.25-ounce box white cake mix
1 cup buttermilk
4 large eggs
¼ cup vegetable oil
1 12-ounce package chocolate chips
1 12-ounce tub chocolate ready-to-spread frosting

1. Preheat oven to 350°F. Line a muffin tin with paper baking cups.

2. Combine cake mix, buttermilk, eggs, and oil, blending completely with an electric mixer. Gently and evenly fold in chocolate chips. Fill each baking cup halfway.

3. Bake 20 minutes. Allow to cool completely before frosting.

# Cherry Cola Cupcakes

*This reintroduced sock-hop favorite taste is reborn in a cupcake. Top with whipped cream and a cherry for a sweet ending to a meal of grilled burgers and hot dogs.*

**INGREDIENTS** | **SERVES 24**

2 eggs

1 teaspoon vanilla

1 18.25-ounce box white cake mix

1¼ cups cherry-flavored cola

1 12-ounce tub ready-made frosting of your choice

1. Preheat oven to 350°F. Line a muffin tin with paper baking cups. Spray lightly with cooking spray.

2. Combine eggs, vanilla, cake mix, and cherry cola in a mixing bowl and mix well using an electric mixer. Bake for 20 minutes. Completely cool cupcakes before frosting.

# Chocolate Chip Red Velvet Cupcakes

*Everyone loves to guard a secret ingredient. This one is surely a treasure. No one will guess that soda pop is the magic-maker in this moist cupcake. Sprinkle just a dusting of cocoa powder on these cupcakes for a decadent extra touch.*

**INGREDIENTS** | **MAKES 24 CUPCAKES**

2 egg whites

1 18.25-ounce box red velvet cake mix

1 12-ounce bag chocolate chips

1 12-ounce can lemon-lime soda pop

1 12-ounce tub ready-to-spread sour cream frosting

1. Preheat oven to 350°F. Line a muffin tin with paper baking cups.

2. Combine egg whites, cake mix, chocolate chips, and soda in a large mixing bowl. Mix well until a smooth batter forms. Pour batter into baking cups.

3. Bake for 20 minutes. Allow cupcakes to cool before frosting.

# All-American Apple Pie Cupcakes

*Plan a trip to an orchard or the farmers' market and make a double batch of
your own pie filling. Use half for a pie and half for these cupcakes.*

**INGREDIENTS | SERVES 24**

1 18.25-ounce box yellow cake mix

¼ cup water

1 egg

2 tablespoons prepared pumpkin pie
spice mix

1 15-ounce can apple pie filling

1 12-ounce tub cream cheese frosting

1. Preheat oven to 350°F. Line a muffin tin with paper
baking cups.

2. Mix cake mix, water, egg, and spice mix with an
electric mixer until a smooth batter forms. Fold in pie
filling. Fill baking cups halfway. Bake for 23 minutes.

3. Allow cupcakes to cool on a rack before frosting.

# Chocolate-Filled Angel Cakes

*This light cake pairs perfectly with a chocolaty crème filling. Serve
with iced tea and fresh fruit on a warm afternoon and enjoy!*

**INGREDIENTS | MAKES 39 CUPCAKES**

1 18.25-ounce box angel food cake mix
plus ingredients called for on box

1 3.9-ounce box instant chocolate
pudding mix plus ingredients called
for on box

1. Preheat oven to 375°F. Line a muffin tin with paper
baking cups.

2. In a large mixing bowl, mix angel food cake
according to the directions on the box. Fill baking
cups ¾ full. Bake for 15 minutes or until golden.

3. Mix pudding according to the directions on the box.

4. Allow cupcakes to cool before using a cookie press to
insert chocolate pudding into the center of the
cupcake.

# Chocolate Sundae Cupcakes

*When you're really ready to pull out the stops, whip up a batch of these decadent delights.*

**INGREDIENTS** | **MAKES 24 CUPCAKES**

1 18-ounce box white cake mix
1 cup buttermilk
¼ cup vegetable oil
4 eggs
1 12-ounce tub vanilla ice cream
Banana slices
Hot fudge ice cream topping
Whipped topping
Sprinkles (optional)
Maraschino cherries

1. Preheat oven to 350°F. Line a muffin tin with paper baking cups.

2. Combine cake mix, buttermilk, oil, and eggs in a large mixing bowl and beat using an electric mixer set to low speed until a smooth batter forms. Fill baking cups halfway.

3. Bake 15 minutes or until tops are golden. Remove from oven and allow to cool completely before frosting.

4. Place each cupcake in a dish and top with a scoop of ice cream, banana slices, fudge topping, whipped topping, sprinkles, and a cherry.

# Fresh Berry Cupcakes

*This eggy, creamy cake topped with light, sweet whipped topping is an amazing way to share and savor sweet, fresh berries. Pick the berries yourself to work up an appetite, or simply walk to the market to buy them fresh.*

**INGREDIENTS** | **MAKES 24 CUPCAKES**

1 18-ounce box white cake mix
1 cup buttermilk
¼ cup vegetable oil
4 eggs
1 16-ounce tub nondairy whipped topping
Fresh berries

1. Preheat oven to 350°F. Line a muffin tin with paper baking cups.

2. Combine all ingredients except whipped topping and berries in a large mixing bowl and combine thoroughly using an electric mixer. Fill baking cups halfway.

3. Bake 15 minutes or until tops are golden. Remove cupcakes from the oven and allow to cool completely. Frost cupcakes with nondairy whipped topping.

4. Top with fresh-sliced berries.

# Grande Ganache Cupcakes

*Ganache belongs not just to the pages of gourmet magazines and ultra-complicated cookbooks. Home cooks can create the taste, too, and with fairly simple ingredients.*

**INGREDIENTS | MAKES 24 CUPCAKES**

1 18-ounce box chocolate cake mix

1 cup buttermilk

¼ cup vegetable oil

4 eggs

1 cup whipping cream

1 12-ounce package bittersweet
   chocolate pieces

1. Preheat oven to 350°F. Line a muffin tin with paper baking cups.

2. Combine cake mix, buttermilk, oil, and eggs in a large mixing bowl and beat using an electric mixer set to low speed until a smooth batter forms. Fill baking cups halfway.

3. Bake about 15 minutes or until tops are golden. Allow cupcakes to cool completely.

4. Meanwhile, to make the ganache, bring whipping cream to a boil in a saucepan over medium heat. Remove pan from heat and add chocolate without stirring.

5. Allow chocolate to melt into cream for 5 minutes. Stir until smooth. Allow to cool for 15 minutes before using to frost cupcakes.

# Carrot Cake Cupcakes

*This favorite cake has lots of healthy tidbits hiding in it. It's a great way to get your vegetables without tasting them.*

**INGREDIENTS | SERVES 24**

¼ cup yellow raisins

¼ cup dark raisins

1 tablespoon hot tap water

1 18.25-ounce box carrot cake mix plus ingredients called for on box

1 cup shredded carrots

½ cup walnuts, chopped

1 12-ounce tub ready-to-spread frosting

1. Combine raisins and hot water. Cover. Set aside.

2. Preheat oven to 350°F. Line a muffin tin with paper baking cups.

3. Prepare batter according to cake mix instructions for cupcakes. Gently fold plumped raisins, shredded carrots, and nuts into batter.

4. Pour batter into muffin tin and bake for the length of time indicated on the package. Allow cupcakes to cool completely before removing from muffin tin.

5. Frost completely cooled cupcakes. Garnish with a piece of shredded carrot.

# Candied Apple Cupcakes

*It's hard to enjoy a caramel apple with a mouth full of dentures or braces.*
*This easy-to-enjoy recipe lets the whole family celebrate autumn without worry.*

**INGREDIENTS | SERVES 12**

1 18.25-ounce box spice cake mix plus
   ingredients called for on box
2 cups apples, finely chopped
20 caramel cubes
3 tablespoons milk

1. Preheat oven to 350°F. Line a muffin tin with paper baking cups.

2. Prepare batter according to cake mix instructions. Fold in chopped apples. Fill baking cups ¾ full. Bake for 20 minutes. Remove from oven and allow to cool.

3. Cook caramels and milk in a double boiler, stirring constantly. Smooth caramel mixture over cupcakes.

# Brownie Cakes

*Not quite a brownie, not quite a cupcake, but definitely the best of both worlds.*
*Pumpkin gives this dessert a lovely texture and flavor with less fat.*

**INGREDIENTS | MAKES 24 CUPCAKES**

1 18.25-ounce box devil's food cake mix
1 15-ounce can pumpkin
⅔ cup water
1 12-ounce tub chocolate frosting

1. Preheat oven to 325°F. Spray muffin tins with nonstick cooking spray.

2. Combine cake mix, pumpkin, and water in a large mixing bowl. Beat using an electric mixer for 2 minutes. Spoon batter into muffin tins. Bake for 40 minutes.

3. Cool cupcakes and frost.

# House Mouse Cupcakes

*Create the sweetest mouse ever in the house and add a little character to your afternoon treat.*

**INGREDIENTS | MAKES 24 CUPCAKES**

1 18.25-ounce box chocolate cake mix plus ingredients called for on box

24 small round chocolate mint cookies, halved

1 12.6-ounce bag round candy-covered chocolates

Thin strings of black licorice

24 scoops chocolate ice cream

1. Preheat oven to 375°F. Line a muffin tin with paper baking cups.

2. Prepare batter and bake according to cake mix instructions for cupcakes. Remove cupcakes from oven and allow to cool completely.

3. Remove cupcakes from paper cups.

4. Using halved round cookies for ears, candies for eyes and nose, and licorice for whiskers, decorate cupcakes to resemble mice. Place on a cookie sheet and freeze.

5. Serve with ice cream.

# Rainy Day Cupcakes

*Sometimes a treat is all about the presentation. This wiggly, colorful treat brightens up a rainy day like few other cupcakes can.*

**INGREDIENTS** | **SERVES 24**

1 18.25-ounce white cake mix plus ingredients called for on box
1 cup boiling water
1 3-ounce box blue gelatin
1 16-ounce tub thawed whipped topping
Blue-colored sugar
Cocktail parasols to decorate

1. Preheat oven to 350°F. Line a muffin tin with paper baking cups.

2. Prepare batter according to cake mix instructions. Spoon batter into cups. Bake according to instructions.

3. Allow cupcakes to cool completely before poking with skewers, creating 8 holes per cupcake. Boil water and dissolve gelatin in it completely.

4. Spoon gelatin over cupcakes so that mixture fills in the holes. Chill cupcakes in the refrigerator for 4 hours so that gelatin sets.

5. Frost with whipped topping and sprinkle with colored sugar. Garnish each cupcake with parasol.

# Pudding-Topped Cupcakes

*The flavors in this treat are simple, familiar, and delicious. Bake them when you need a taste of childhood.*

**INGREDIENTS | MAKES 12 CUPCAKES**

1 18.25-ounce box cake mix plus ingredients called for on box

1 cup milk

1 3.9-ounce package instant pudding mix

3½ cups nondairy whipped topping

1. Prepare and bake cupcakes according to cake mix instructions.

2. Combine milk and pudding mix in a large mixing bowl, whisking to blend. Fold in whipped topping and combine thoroughly.

3. Use pudding mixture to frost completely cooled cupcakes.

# Whipping Cream

*Whipped topping is great when you're in a hurry, but for a super-luscious treat make your own whipped cream. It's easy!*

**INGREDIENTS | 1 CUP**

1 cup whipping cream

½ tablespoon vanilla

2 tablespoons sugar

Add all ingredients to a chilled mixing bowl. Beat with an electric mixer set to medium speed until you reach the desired consistency.

# Strawberry Cheese Cupcakes

*The light, sweet richness of mascarpone adds a European touch to this otherwise simple cupcake. This recipe would work with any flavor of jam. Get creative. Try seasonal favorites.*

**INGREDIENTS | MAKES 24 CUPCAKES**

1 18.25-ounce box white cake mix
2 cups mascarpone cheese
2 eggs
⅓ cup strawberry preserves

1. Preheat oven to 350°F. Line a muffin tin with paper baking cups.

2. Combine all ingredients except preserves in a large mixing bowl and mix well using a wooden spoon. Fill baking cups halfway, reserving about ⅓ of the batter.

3. Drop ½ teaspoon preserves into the center of each cupcake and then cover with remaining batter.

4. Bake for 25 minutes or until cupcakes spring back when gently touched. Cool cupcakes on wire racks.

# Berry Crème Cupcakes

*There are no artificial colors in this sweet pink dessert. Try it with different berries to get different hues and different tastes.*

**INGREDIENTS | MAKES 24 CUPCAKES**

1 16-ounce package frozen strawberries

1 18.25-ounce box white cake mix

3 egg whites

2 tablespoons vegetable oil

1 16-ounce tub nondairy whipped topping

1. Thaw frozen berries, drain package, and reserve liquid.

2. Preheat oven to 350°F. Line a muffin tin with paper baking cups.

3. Combine cake mix, egg whites, and oil in a large bowl and beat with an electric mixer until a smooth batter forms. Fold in drained berries. Fill baking cups halfway.

4. Bake for 19 minutes. Remove from oven. As cupcakes cool, mix strawberry liquid and whipped topping. Top completely cool cupcakes with this mixture.

# CHAPTER 11

# For Chocolate Lovers

# Ultra-Chocolate Cake

*This simply sweet chocolate cake is a great foundation for other recipes.*
*It can be embellished with nuts or bits of candy.*

**INGREDIENTS | SERVES 8**

1 3.9-ounce package chocolate pudding plus ingredients called for on box

1 18.25-ounce box chocolate cake mix

½ cup semisweet chocolate chips

½ cup sweetened shaved coconut (optional)

Whipped topping

1. Preheat oven to 350°F. Grease a cake pan. Set aside.

2. Make pudding according to package instructions. While pudding is still hot, blend in dry cake mix.

3. Blend with a whisk or an electric mixer until batter is free of lumps. Turn batter into pan.

4. Layer chocolate chips and coconut onto batter. Bake for 35 minutes. Serve warm with whipped topping.

# Rich Chocolate Bundt Cake

*Consider a side of strawberries, raspberries, or whipped topping*
*to bring out the chocolate flavors in this cake.*

**INGREDIENTS | SERVES 12**

1 18.25-ounce box devil's food cake mix

1 3.9-ounce box instant chocolate pudding

2 cups sour cream

5 eggs

1 teaspoon almond extract

1 cup butter, melted

2 cups semisweet chocolate chips

1. Preheat oven to 350°F. Grease a bundt pan. Set aside.

2. In a large mixing bowl, blend cake mix, pudding mix, sour cream, eggs, extract, and butter with an electric mixer set to medium speed.

3. Gently fold in chocolate chips with a wooden spoon. Turn batter into the pan. Bake for 50 minutes. Cool cake before inverting onto wire rack.

# Chocolate Upside-Down Cake

*On the surface, this is a simple chocolate sheet cake, but underneath*
*it's a gooey, luscious, chocolate delight.*

**INGREDIENTS** | **SERVES 12**

1 cup sweetened flaked coconut

1 cup chopped nuts

1 18.25-ounce box German chocolate cake mix

⅓ cup olive oil

1¼ cups water

3 eggs

1 pound confectioners' sugar

1 cup margarine

1 8-ounce package cream cheese

1 cup semisweet chocolate chips

1. Preheat oven to 375°F. Grease a 13" × 9" inch pan. Layer coconut and nuts in the pan, evenly covering the bottom.

2. Mix cake mix, oil, water, and eggs in a large mixing bowl using an electric mixer set to medium speed. Stop when the batter is smooth and free of lumps.

3. Spoon batter over coconut and nuts. Bake for 45 minutes or until a toothpick comes out clean.

4. As cake bakes, mix confectioners' sugar, margarine, and cream cheese in a mixing bowl. Beat mixture with an electric mixer until light and smooth.

5. When cake is baked, remove from oven and invert onto a serving dish. Frost with cream cheese mixture and sprinkle with chocolate chips.

# Classic Chocolate Trifle

*This traditional favorite is picture perfect and lovely when served in a footed glass bowl—but that's not the only way to do it. Try different food-safe glass containers. Get creative.*

**INGREDIENTS | SERVES 12**

1 18.25-ounce box chocolate cake mix plus ingredients called for on box

1 3.9-ounce box instant chocolate pudding plus ingredients called for on box

1 8-ounce tub whipped topping

4 toffee or solid chocolate candy bars

1. Prepare and bake cake according to cake mix instructions. Cool cake. Cut into cubes.

2. Make instant pudding according to instructions on the package; cool.

3. Break candy into small pieces.

4. Layer half the cake cubes in the glass bowl. Follow with half the pudding. Add half the whipped topping and top with half the candy. Repeat one more time to fill bowl.

5. Chill until ready to serve.

# Chocolate Sandwich Cookies

*For an extra-fancy finish roll the cookies through a saucer filled with colored sugar or sprinkles. The sprinkles will stick to the filling and create a fun decorative strip.*

**INGREDIENTS | SERVES 10**

1 18.25-ounce box chocolate cake mix

1 egg, room temperature

½ cup butter

1 12-ounce tub vanilla frosting

1. Preheat oven to 350°F. Cover a cookie sheet with a layer of parchment paper. Set aside.

2. In a large mixing bowl, combine cake mix, egg, and butter. Use an electric mixer to create a smooth, uniform batter.

3. Roll cookie dough into 1" balls and place them on cookie sheet. Press each ball with a spoon to flatten. Bake for 10 minutes.

4. Allow cookies to cool completely before sandwiching a layer of frosting between two cookies.

# Cocoa-Cola Cake

*The orange extract tucked in the mix adds a fragrant sweetness that sings of spring. Consider sugared orange rinds to decorate this cake. Cut them into small pieces and sprinkle them on the cake or use the curved whole rinds to create designs in the frosting.*

**INGREDIENTS | SERVES 12**

1 18.25-ounce box devil's food cake mix
3 eggs
1⅓ cups cola
½ cup olive oil
1 tablespoon orange extract
1 teaspoon vanilla extract
Frosting

1. Preheat oven to 350°F. Grease a cake pan. Set aside.

2. In a large bowl, combine cake mix, eggs, cola, oil, orange extract, and vanilla extract. Beat with an electric mixer set to medium speed to form a smooth batter.

3. Pour batter into cake pan. Bake for 30 minutes or until a toothpick comes out clean. Cool cake on a wire rack before frosting.

# Hot Chocolate Cake

*Mix cake batter and bake it in your favorite mugs. They're easy to hold and eat.*

**INGREDIENTS | SERVES 12**

1 18.25-ounce box chocolate cake mix plus ingredients called for on box
1 16-ounce tub frozen whipped topping
Sprinkles or small marshmallows for garnish

### Mexican Mocha

For an unexpected flavor add an octagon of Mexican hot chocolate, which you can find in the world food section of most grocery stores. Melt the chocolate in the milk you plan to add to the batter. The cinnamon and other spices will add a warming, unexpected flavor.

1. Preheat oven to 350°F. Butter 12 oven-safe mugs.

2. Mix cake batter according to cake mix instructions for cupcakes. Pour batter into mugs. Bake according to instructions for cupcakes.

3. Remove from oven and serve warm with a generous dollop of whipped topping. Garnish with sprinkles or marshmallows.

# Micro-Mug Cake for One

*Mix the batter and refrigerate it. Then microwave a cake in your favorite mug whenever you want a warm sweet treat.*

**INGREDIENTS | SERVES 12**

1 18.25-ounce box chocolate cake mix plus ingredients called for on box

Marshmallow fluff

1. Mix batter according to instructions on the package; put in an airtight container and refrigerate.

2. Fill a mug halfway full with batter. Microwave on high for 3 minutes. Remove and dot with marshmallow fluff. Allow to stand 2 minutes before eating.

# Sweet Layers Chocolate Cake

*When creating poke cakes, work with the idea of creating a waffle-like top in the cake. The point is to poke holes that allow liquid to soak into the cake completely.*

**INGREDIENTS | SERVES 12**

1 18.25-ounce box chocolate cake mix plus ingredients called for on box

1 6-ounce jar caramel ice cream topping

1 7-ounce can unsweetened condensed milk

1 8-ounce tub nondairy whipped topping, thawed

8 candy bars, chopped or broken into bits

1. Prepare and bake cake according to instructions for a 9" × 13" cake.

2. Remove cake from oven and let cool for 10 minutes before poking holes in the top of the cake with a long-pronged fork or skewer.

3. Pour caramel and then condensed milk over cake, filling all the holes. Let the cake stand until it has cooled completely.

4. Frost with whipped topping and sprinkle with candy bar pieces. Refrigerate until ready to serve.

# Lower-Fat Chocolate Cake

*This lower-fat recipe saves calories on the butter and oil, allowing you to savor a slice of cake without guilt. For a low-fat frosting, combine fat-free instant pudding and fat-free whipped topping. Frost the cake and chill before serving.*

**INGREDIENTS | SERVES 12**

1 18.25-ounce box chocolate cake mix

⅓ cup low-fat applesauce

1¼ cups water

1 12-ounce tub low-fat prepared frosting or whipped topping

1. Preheat oven to 350°F. Grease and flour cake pan. Set aside.

2. Mix all ingredients in a large mixing bowl for 2 minutes using an electric mixer. Turn batter into pan. Bake according to cake mix instructions.

3. Cool cake before frosting.

# Crock-o-Late Cake

*A slow cooker pot can be a valuable helper on a busy day. Just mix your recipe, pop it in the slow cooker, and go about your day. When you come home, a warm cake will be waiting for you and the house will smell fantastic.*

**INGREDIENTS | SERVES 12**

1 18.25-ounce box chocolate cake mix

1 2-ounce package instant chocolate pudding

4 eggs

1 cup water

2 cups sour cream

¾ cups vegetable oil

1 cup semisweet chocolate chips

1. Grease a 4-quart slow cooker.

2. In a medium bowl, mix cake and pudding mixes. In a large bowl, mix eggs, water, sour cream, and oil.

3. Slowly add the dry ingredients to the wet ingredients as you beat the batter with an electric mixer set on medium speed. Add chocolate chips and stir by hand to thoroughly incorporate.

4. Turn batter into slow cooker. Cover and cook on low for 6 hours. Cake is done if it springs back when lightly touched. If it doesn't, cook in 15-minute increments until it is done.

# Sandwich Cookie Cake

*This cake can't be dunked in a glass of milk, but it's just as tasty as your favorite sandwich cookies. The creamy filling is the sweet note that makes this cake a special event in and of itself.*

**INGREDIENTS | SERVES 12**

1 18.25-ounce box devil's food cake mix

1 3.9-ounce box instant chocolate pudding

1 cup vegetable oil

1 cup sour cream

4 eggs

½ cup skim milk

2 teaspoons vanilla extract

2 cups mini semisweet chocolate chips

Sandwich Cookie Cake Frosting (page 177)

1. Preheat oven to 350°F. Grease and flour cake pans. Set aside.

2. In a large mixing bowl, combine all ingredients except chocolate chips and frosting, mixing with an electric mixer on medium until batter is entirely smooth.

3. Fold in chocolate chips. Turn batter into two round cake pans. Bake for 45 minutes or until a toothpick comes out clean.

4. As cake bakes, mix one batch of Sandwich Cookie Cake Frosting.

5. Remove cake from oven and allow to cool before turning one layer onto the serving platter. Spread the top of this first layer with a generous helping of frosting.

6. Invert the second layer on top of the frosting, creating a sandwich. Use the rest of the frosting to cover the cake.

# Sandwich Cookie Cake Frosting

*The best part of the sandwich cookie is the crème filling. A batch of this creamy frosting adds that beautiful layer of sweetness to your chocolate confection.*

**INGREDIENTS | SERVES 12**

1 cup solid vegetable shortening

4½ cups confectioners' sugar

¼ teaspoon sea salt

2 teaspoons vanilla extract

⅓ cup unsweetened, heavy whipping cream

1. In a stainless steel mixing bowl, using an electric mixer set to medium speed, beat vegetable shortening until light and fluffy. Slowly add sugar and continue to beat.

2. Add salt, vanilla extract, and whipping cream, continuing to beat. Turn the electric mixer to high speed and beat until light and fluffy. Frost your cake.

# Coconaise Cake

*Mayonnaise is a great way to add light egg and oil to your recipe. Try it for a rich, light crumb that doesn't taste like a mix cake. Serve this cake with fresh raspberries or strawberries. The flavors complement chocolate famously, and the lightness of the fruit is lovely with the richness of the cake.*

**INGREDIENTS | SERVES 12**

1 box chocolate cake mix

1 cup mayonnaise

1 cup water

3 eggs

1 teaspoon ground cinnamon

2 tablespoons cocoa powder

1 12-ounce tub prepared chocolate frosting

1. Preheat the oven to 350°F. Grease and flour cake pans. Set aside.

2. Combine cake mix, mayonnaise, water, eggs, cinnamon, and cocoa powder in a large mixing bowl. Beat batter smooth with an electric mixer set to medium speed.

3. Turn cake batter into pans. Bake for 25 minutes or until fork comes out clean. Allow cake to cool completely before frosting.

# Movie Night Brownies

*There's no secret to this simple recipe. With just four ingredients and only a few easy steps, they're quick enough to whip up while the previews are playing. You can frost them, sprinkle them with confectioners' sugar, or serve them with a scoop of ice cream.*

**INGREDIENTS** | **SERVES 12**

1 3.9-ounce package instant vanilla pudding plus ingredients called for on box

2 cups whole milk

1 18.25-ounce box chocolate cake mix without pudding

2 cups semisweet chocolate chips

1. Preheat oven to 350°F.

2. Make pudding, whisking to combine thoroughly.

3. Slowly add cake mix to the pudding mixture. Fold in chocolate chips. Turn batter into a jellyroll pan and bake for 15 to 20 minutes.

4. Allow to cool slightly before cutting into bars.

# Chocolate Cake Batter Ice Cream

*This is a great way to enjoy the taste of fresh cake batter and homemade ice cream. It's easy to do with an ice-cream maker. Serve with whipped cream, chocolate syrup, or both! Top with fruit or sprinkles for an extra-special presentation.*

**INGREDIENTS** | **SERVES 8**

1 cup whole milk, chilled

¾ cup sugar

2 cups whipping cream, chilled

1 teaspoon vanilla extract

⅔ cup cake mix

1. Whisk milk and sugar together in a stainless steel mixing bowl until well incorporated. Add whipping cream and vanilla extract. Continue to whisk.

2. Slowly add cake mix, whisking to avoid lumps. Put mixture in an ice-cream maker and continue according to manufacturer's instructions.

# Malt Shoppe Chocolate Cake

*Love a malt? This is the cake that captures the flavor. Serve with a
shake or vanilla ice cream for that malt shop, sock-hop flavor.*

**INGREDIENTS | SERVES 14**

1 18.25-ounce box chocolate cake mix
1 cup malted milk powder
1⅓ cups water
3 eggs
½ cup butter, softened
½ gallon ice cream, softened
1 16-ounce jar hot fudge ice cream
    topping
1 cup malted milk balls

1. Preheat oven to 350°F. Grease cake pans. Set aside.

2. Combine dry cake mix and malted milk powder in a
   large mixing bowl and whisk to combine completely.
   Slowly add water, eggs, and butter.

3. Beat batter for 1 minute using an electric mixer set to
   medium speed. Turn batter into cake pans. Bake for
   40 minutes or until a toothpick comes out clean.

4. Allow cakes to cool completely. Mark the center of the
   cake with toothpicks all the way around. Using the
   toothpicks as your guide, cut the cake in half
   horizontally.

5. Line a cake pan with plastic wrap. Alternate layers of
   cake and softened ice cream to fill pan. Wrap in
   plastic wrap and freeze until ready to serve.

6. Garnish with hot fudge and malted milk balls.

# Turtle Skillet Cakes

*These griddle cakes aren't for breakfast, but they're a perfect treat for pajama parties or snowy nights. Cuddle up with these and a cup of something warm for a decadent delight.*

**INGREDIENTS | SERVES 14**

1 18.25-ounce box devil's food cake mix plus ingredients called for on box

1 tablespoon butter

4 1-ounce pieces semisweet baking chocolate

1 12-ounce jar caramel ice cream topping

Whipped topping

## Equipment

Some recipes call for elaborate baking equipment, but this recipe uses something you probably already have: a skillet. This method of baking will work on many basic cake recipes. If you're just learning to bake and aren't ready to invest in expensive equipment, try making this recipe in a thin-walled skillet.

1. Preheat oven to 350°F.

2. Make cake batter according to cake mix instructions.

3. Melt butter in an oven-safe iron or nonstick skillet over medium heat. Gently tilt the skillet to make sure the butter covers the bottom of the pan.

4. Turn batter into the skillet and bake in the oven, uncovered, for 30 minutes. Remove skillet from oven and allow cake to cool.

5. Run a knife around the edge of the pan to loosen cake slightly. Then invert the pan onto the cooling rack and allow the cake to fall free.

6. Grate, shave, or chop the chocolate into small pieces. In a small microwave-safe bowl, mix chocolate pieces and half the caramel topping.

7. Microwave the chocolate/caramel mix for 40 seconds or until melted. Stir. Pour over cake. Add a thin layer of reserved caramel sauce. Top with whipped topping.

# Chocolaty Coconut Cake

*Sure, there are other chocolate cake recipes, but how many of them offer the combination of moistening pudding and rich coconut? Serve this with warm tea or hot cocoa.*

**INGREDIENTS | SERVES 12**

1 18.25-ounce box devil's food cake mix plus ingredients called for on box

1 3.9-ounce box instant chocolate pudding

1 cup milk

1 16-ounce tub whipped topping, thawed

Mini semisweet chocolate chips

½ cup sweetened, flaked coconut

## Keep Your Cool

Cakes frosted with whipped topping hold their shape and their frosting better if they stay refrigerated. Not only do they hold consistency better; they also remain easy to slice. Drizzle with chocolate syrup for an extra-rich decorative touch.

1. Preheat oven to 350°F.

2. Mix cake batter according to cake mix instructions. Pour batter into a bundt pan and bake according to instructions.

3. Meanwhile, in a medium-sized stainless steel bowl, whisk pudding mix and milk together for 2 minutes. Fold in whipped topping and chocolate chips.

4. Remove cake from oven and let cool completely before inverting onto a serving platter. Frost cake with whipped topping mixture. Sprinkle with coconut.

# Chocolate Zucchini Cake

*Zucchini adds moistness and texture to your chocolate cake. Bake this every year when the garden harvest comes in or after your first trip to the farmers' market.*

**INGREDIENTS** | **SERVES 12**

¾ cup butter, softened

3 eggs

1 teaspoon vanilla extract

¼ teaspoon almond extract

1 cup sour cream

1 18.25-ounce box chocolate cake mix with pudding

1 medium zucchini, grated

1 12-ounce tub prepared chocolate frosting

1. Preheat oven to 325°F. Grease and flour a bundt pan. Set aside.

2. In a large mixing bowl, cream butter, eggs, vanilla extract, and almond extract. Slowly incorporate the sour cream. Add cake mix. Fold in grated zucchini.

3. Spoon batter into the cake pan and shake until batter is level. Bake 45 minutes or until a toothpick comes out clean.

4. Cool cake completely before inverting pan onto serving platter. Frost cake with prepared frosting.

## Zucchini Peels

Some cooks peel zucchini before grating, but others maintain that the peel contains most of the nutrients. Both are perfectly acceptable. If, however, you decide to use the peel in your cake, please take the time to thoroughly wash the zucchini. Conventional farming can leave pesticides and waxes on the squash that you may not want in your cake.

# Mexican Chocolate Cake

*South of the border, people add a little spice to their cocoa. Cinnamon is the secret ingredient, but some cooks also add a quick and very scant dash of cayenne pepper for heat.*

**INGREDIENTS | SERVES 12**

1 18.25-ounce box chocolate cake mix
1 teaspoon cinnamon
1½ cups water
½ cup vegetable oil
4 eggs
1 cup semisweet chocolate chips
3 tablespoons butter

## Condensed Milk Caramel

Boil a pot of water. Remove the label (but not the lid) from a can of sweetened condensed milk and boil the can for 20 minutes, keeping the pot covered. Reduce the heat and simmer, still covered, for 90 minutes. Allow the can to cool, remove the lid, and drizzle the caramel over the cake.

1. Preheat oven to 350°F. Grease and flour a bundt pan. Set aside.

2. In a large mixing bowl combine cake mix, cinnamon, water, oil, and eggs. Combine with an electric mixer. Fold in chocolate chips. Pour into pan.

3. Bake for 35 minutes or until a toothpick comes out clean. Drizzle warm cake with Condensed Milk Caramel.

# Chocolate Latte Cake

*Skip the coffee shop and enjoy the sophisticated flavor of a latte fresh from your own oven. The ingredients are simple, but the results are stellar.*

**INGREDIENTS | SERVES 12**

2 tablespoons butter

1½ cups graham cracker crumbs

1 18.25-ounce box devil's food cake mix

¾ cup semisweet chocolate morsels

1½ cups whipping cream

1½ teaspoons instant coffee crystals

⅓ cup confectioners' sugar

1. Preheat oven to 350°F. Grease and flour cake pans. Set aside.

2. Mix melted butter and graham cracker crumbs and set aside to cool.

3. Prepare cake batter according to cake mix instructions for a two-layer cake. Pour into two cake pans.

4. Sprinkle butter/crumb mixture and chocolate morsels over batter before baking. Bake for 35 minutes. Remove from oven and allow to cool.

5. In a stainless steel bowl, beat whipping cream, instant coffee crystals, and confectioners' sugar until stiff peaks form.

6. Turn one layer of cake onto a serving plate. Spread cream mixture on top and sides. Add top layer and frost remainder of cake with cream mixture. Chill until ready to serve.

# Peanut Butter Fudge Brownies

*Cake mix makes chewy and thick brownies with a wonderful flavor. The ground chocolate adds creaminess. Be careful to not overbake these brownies.*

**INGREDIENTS | SERVES 36**

1 18.25-ounce package dark chocolate cake mix

½ cup dark chocolate chips, ground

½ cup peanut butter

2 eggs

¼ cup water

1 16-ounce tub ready to spread vanilla frosting

⅓ cup peanut butter

2 cups powdered sugar

¼ cup cocoa

3 tablespoons water

¼ cup peanut butter

¼ cup butter

1 teaspoon vanilla

1. Preheat oven to 350°F. Spray a 13" × 9" pan with nonstick baking spray containing flour and set aside. In large bowl, combine cake mix, ground chocolate, ½ cup peanut butter, eggs, and water and mix until combined. Beat for 40 strokes, then spread into prepared pan.

2. Bake for 26–31 minutes or until brownies are just set. Cool completely on wire rack.

3. In same bowl, combine powdered sugar and cocoa and mix well. In small microwave-safe bowl, combine water, peanut butter, and butter; microwave on high until butter melts, about 1 minute. Pour into powdered sugar mixture, add vanilla, and beat until smooth.

4. Immediately pour over peanut butter filling and gently spread to cover. Let stand until frosting is firm, then cut into bars.

# Chocolate Angel Cakes

*This fabulous recipe tastes like a scratch cake. The little cakes are still a*
*lot of work, but cake mix and ready-made frosting help a lot.*

**INGREDIENTS** | **YIELDS 20 CAKES**

1 18.25-ounce package chocolate cake mix

1 cup water

⅓ cup oil

2 eggs

¾ cup semisweet chocolate chips, ground

3 16-ounce cans ready to spread chocolate frosting

2–3 cups finely chopped pecans

## Flavor Variations

You can change the flavor of this simple recipe in many ways. Use white cake mix, white chocolate chips, and white frosting. A spice cake can be used, also with white chocolate chips and butter frosting. Or mix and match; make a white cake and frost it with chocolate frosting. You get the idea!

1. Preheat oven to 350°F. Spray a 9" × 13" pan with nonstick baking spray containing flour and set aside.

2. In large bowl, combine cake mix, water, oil, and eggs and blend. Beat two minutes at high speed. Fold in the finely ground chocolate chips. Spread into prepared pan.

3. Bake for 35–45 minutes or until toothpick inserted in cake comes out clean. Let cake cool completely on wire rack.

4. Cut cake into 20 pieces and remove from pan, one at a time. Frost the little cakes on all sides and roll in the chopped pecans to coat.

# Mocha Mud Bundt Cake

*This is a sophisticated cake for the latte-lovers in your life. As with all bundt cakes, this is easy to make and easy to carry.*

**INGREDIENTS | SERVES 12**

1 18.25-ounce box cake mix

4 eggs

½ cup vegetable oil

1 16-ounce tub sour cream

½ cup Kahlua

1 8-ounce package semisweet chocolate chips

Whipped topping for garnish

Nutmeg for garnish

1. Preheat oven to 350°F. Grease a bundt pan and set aside.

2. Mix together cake mix, eggs, oil, sour cream, and Kahlua. Mix until batter is smooth. Fold in chocolate chips. Turn batter into cake pan.

3. Bake for 1 hour. When the cake is done, the top will spring back after being touched lightly. Allow cake to cool slightly before inverting onto serving platter.

4. Garnish with whipped topping and sprinkles of nutmeg.

## CHAPTER 12

# Holiday Favorites

# Fruitcake

*Fruitcakes are best when flavors are allowed to mingle. Traditionally, cakes would age for weeks in a dark, cool closet. You don't need to go that far. A day or two in your nice, clean fridge will work wonders! Use fruit-flavored brandy if possible.*

**INGREDIENTS | SERVES 8**

**Fruitcake**

1 18.25-ounce box yellow cake mix
1 3.9-ounce box vanilla pudding mix
⅔ cup pineapple juice
¼ cup brandy
½ cup vegetable oil
4 large eggs
1 cup pecans, crushed
1 cup chopped dates
½ cup chopped maraschino cherries
½ cup chopped candied pineapple
Whole pecans for garnish

**Glaze**

1 cup confectioners' sugar
2 to 3 tablespoons brandy

1. Preheat oven to 350°F. Grease and flour a 10" tube pan. Set aside.

2. Pour cake mix into a bowl. Fold in pudding mix, pineapple juice, brandy, and oil. Mix for 3 minutes or until batter is smooth. Add eggs, beating continuously.

3. Stir in pecans and all fruit. Pour batter into cake pan. Top with a few whole pecans. Bake for 50 minutes or until a fork comes out clean.

4. Cool for 15 minutes in the pan, then remove to a rack to cool thoroughly. Mix Glaze and drizzle over cooled cake. Cover in plastic wrap and age in refrigerator for one or two days.

# Rum Cake

*This variation on a favorite rum cake is a little less boozy than the original, but you can add more if you like. Not all of the alcohol will bake out of this recipe, so people sensitive to alcohol should proceed with caution. Top with Rum Cake Glaze (page 192).*

**INGREDIENTS | SERVES 12**

1 cup chopped walnuts
1 18.25-ounce box yellow cake mix
1 3.9-ounce box instant vanilla pudding mix
4 eggs
½ cup milk
½ cup canola oil
¼ cup Bacardi dark rum

1. Preheat oven to 325°F. Generously grease and flour a bundt pan, even if it is nonstick. Set aside.

2. Generously layer nuts in the bottom of the pan. (When liquid batter is added, they'll float to the top.)

3. Beat together cake mix, pudding mix, eggs, milk, oil and dark rum for 3 minutes. Turn batter into the bundt pan. Gently bang pan on counter to even out batter.

4. Bake for 1 hour. Remove from oven and let cake rest in bundt pan for 2 hours. When cake is cool, turn it out onto a platter.

# Rum Cake Glaze

*You could make the cake without the glaze, but why would you? It's where the rummy yummy lives! A dollop of whipped topping is the perfecting touch.*

**INGREDIENTS | YIELDS 1 CUP**

½ cup butter
¼ cup water
1 cup sugar
½ cup dark rum

1. Melt butter in a saucepan over low heat. Slowly whisk in water and sugar. Bring to a boil; boil for 5 minutes. Remove pan from burner and stir in rum, using a spoon with a long handle.

2. Poke holes in the baked Rum Cake with a wooden skewer or long-pronged fork.

3. Pour glaze generously into holes, just as you would syrup into the holes of a waffle.

## Cozy Cakes

For a traditional taste, wrap the rum cake in cheesecloth and let it set for a few days. The longer the cake rests, the better it is. For exactly this reason, it's the perfect addition for a care package.

# Minute Macaroons

*These are great for the holidays and any other time hungry friends gather together. They are very portable, so keep this recipe top of mind when planning for potlucks.*

**INGREDIENTS | MAKES 20 MACAROONS**

1 18-ounce box vanilla cake mix
⅓ cup butter
2 tablespoons room-temperature water
1 teaspoon vanilla extract
1 egg, slightly beaten
1½ cups sweetened flaked coconut
½ cup dark chocolate chips

1. Preheat oven to 350°F. Lightly butter a 13" × 9" pan and set aside.

2. Pour cake mix into a large bowl. Crumble butter into mix until fully incorporated. Stir in water. Mix in vanilla. Add egg and gently fold in coconut. Turn into cake pan.

3. Bake for 18 minutes. Let cool for 20 minutes. Melt chocolate chips in a warm double boiler or small saucepan. Drizzle over top of cookies. Chill for 2 hours. Cut into bars.

# Cherry Sugar Plums

*These sweet, fruity, nutty treats are easy, economical, and a hit at cookie swaps and holiday parties everywhere. Substitute grenadine for water in this recipe for an extra cherry kick.*

**INGREDIENTS | MAKES 24 COOKIES**

1 18-ounce box cherry cake mix
2 eggs
½ cup butter
1 tablespoon water
¼ cup walnuts, chopped
Confectioners' sugar

1. Combine all ingredients except confectioners' sugar in a bowl. Spoon into 1" balls. Chill in the refrigerator for 2 hours. Preheat oven to 375°F.

2. Remove cookies from fridge. Place confectioners' sugar in a paper bag and add cookies. Shake very gently to coat. Place onto an ungreased cookie sheet by spoonfuls. Bake for 12 minutes. Cool on rack.

# Kitschy Pixie Poke Cake

*Get out your pixie ornaments and your Chipmunks albums. This tried, true, and much-loved recipe will transport you to a time when it was chic to bake with gelatin dessert mix!*

**INGREDIENTS | SERVES 12**

1 18.25-ounce white cake mix plus ingredients called for on box

2 cups boiling water, divided

1 3-ounce box cherry or strawberry gelatin dessert

1 3-ounce box lime gelatin dessert

1 9-ounce tub whipped topping

## Versatile Holiday Treat

Use red, white, and blue gelatin for an Independence Day party or pink and green gelatin for a Southern-style sorority get-together. This cake is a crowd pleaser, and it can be adjusted to fit almost any event simply by choosing the appropriate color of gelatin.

1. Bake cake according to instructions on box for layer cake. Remove from oven and allow cake to cool.

2. Pierce layers with skewers or fork either at regular intervals or in a pattern of your choice.

3. Mix 1 cup boiling water with red gelatin; stir until completely dissolved. Pour over one pierced cake layer. Repeat with green gelatin; pour over the other layer.

4. Chill both layers for 4 hours or overnight. Rest cake pans in a shallow container of warm water. Once warm, invert one layer onto a serving plate. Frost with half of the whipped topping. Repeat with remaining layer.

5. Chill for 2 hours. Decorate cake and top with an ornament if desired.

# Day-Glo Valentine Cake

*Give a big beautiful valentine to someone special this year! This brightly colored Valentine's Day treat is sure to get some love. The brighter the gelatin and food coloring you use, the better.*

**INGREDIENTS | SERVES 12**

1 18-ounce box white cake mix
1 3-ounce package instant gelatin
1 cup milk
3 large eggs
½ cup butter, melted
2 teaspoons vanilla extract
1 tub prepared white frosting
Food coloring

1. Preheat oven to 350°F. Generously butter and flour two cake pans: one round (9") and one square (9"). Set aside.

2. Combine cake mix, gelatin, milk, eggs, butter, and vanilla extract with an electric mixer on low speed.

3. Increase speed to medium and beat for an additional 3 minutes or until batter is free of lumps and completely blended.

4. Pour batter into pans and bake according to box instructions for two layers. Remove cakes from oven and invert onto cooling racks.

5. Allow cakes to cool to room temperature. Place square cake on serving surface so that it looks like a diamond.

6. Cut the round layer in half and place the halves on either side of the diamond's upper edges to make a heart. Combine frosting and food coloring. Frost cake.

# Chocolate-Covered-Cherry Brownies

*This dessert boasts all the decadence of chocolate-covered cherries in a rich, chewy, easy-to-bake brownie!*

**INGREDIENTS | MAKES 9 BROWNIES**

1 18.25-ounce box of the most decadent brownie mix you can find plus ingredients called for on box (except for liquid)

1 6-ounce jar of maraschino cherries

1 1.55-ounce bar dark chocolate

1. Prepare brownies according to the directions on the box, substituting the liquid from the jar of cherries for the liquid called for in the cake mix instructions. If there isn't enough liquid from the cherries, add water to reach desired amount.

2. Top with maraschino cherries and squares of chocolate. Bake according to instructions on box. Let cool.

# Green Beer Cake

*What's more St. Patrick's Day than green beer? Nothing! This cake can almost certainly drive the snakes out of Ireland, but just in case it can't, raise a pint to good St. Patrick and enjoy the day!*

**INGREDIENTS | SERVES 12**

1 18-ounce box yellow cake mix

1 3.9-ounce package instant vanilla pudding mix

1 cup beer

Green food coloring

¼ cup vegetable oil

4 eggs

Frosting

1. Preheat oven to 350°F. Grease and flour a 10" bundt pan. Set aside.

2. Blend cake mix and pudding mix in a large bowl with a wooden spoon. Color beer as green as you like using green food coloring. Stir beer and oil into batter.

3. Add eggs. Beat mixture with electric mixer set to high speed. When mixture is thick and creamy, pour into pan. Bake for 55 minutes.

4. Cool in pan for 15 minutes. Invert cake onto cooling rack. Cool cake completely. Frost as desired.

# Leprechaun Cupcakes

*These green snacks are too cute for words! They're easy to whip up for a St. Patrick's Day party.*

**INGREDIENTS** | **MAKES 24 CUPCAKES**

1 package white cake mix

4 eggs

1 cup vegetable oil

1 cup lemon-lime soda

1 3.9-ounce package pistachio instant pudding mix

1 batch Top o' the Cupcake to You Icing (below)

1. Preheat oven to 350°F. Line a muffin tin with paper baking cups. Set aside.

2. Mix all ingredients except frosting in a large bowl. Beat together for 3 minutes with an electric beater set on medium speed. Fill muffin cups ½ full. Bake for 30 minutes.

3. Cool completely. Remove from muffin pan. Frost and serve.

# Top o' the Cupcake to You Icing

*Even cupcakes like to participate in the wearing o' the green on St. Patrick's day.*
*Dress yours up in the luck of the Irish and take a big, sweet bite.*

**INGREDIENTS** | **MAKES 1½ CUPS**

1 3.9-ounce package pistachio instant pudding mix

1½ cups milk

1 8-ounce container nondairy whipped cream

Mix pudding and milk for 2 minutes using electric mixer on low speed. Fold in nondairy whipped topping.

# Sparkling Lavender Garden Party Cupcakes

*The light citrus flavor and glittery magical sprinkles make these cupcakes perfect for tea parties.*

**INGREDIENTS | MAKES 24 CUPCAKES**

Juice of 1 lemon

Water

1 18-ounce box lemon-flavored cake mix

¼ cup vegetable oil

3 eggs

2 tablespoons lavender buds (reserve a small amount for garnish)

Zest of 1 lemon

1 16-ounce tub white frosting

Candied lemon peel for garnish

Pink sprinkles for garnish

1. Preheat oven to temperature specified in cake mix instructions. Line a muffin tin with paper baking cups. Set aside.

2. Combine lemon juice and enough water to reach amount of water called for in the cake mix instructions.

3. Empty dry cake mix into a large mixing bowl. Add water/juice, oil, eggs, most of lavender buds, and lemon zest to taste. Beat for 2 minutes using a mixer set to high speed.

4. Fill muffin cups ½ full. Bake according to the cake mix instructions. Remove cupcakes from oven when they are just slightly brown around the edges.

5. Frost while warm so that frosting melts to a glaze. Sprinkle with a few lavender buds. Add candied lemon peel for garnish. Dust with sprinkles.

# Easter Coconut Cake

*You can re-create the taste of the classic Betty Crocker Easter Bunny Cake with this simple coconut cake recipe. Decorate it with Easter candy for a cake so sweet you'll forget what's in your basket.*

**INGREDIENTS | SERVES 12**

1 18.25-ounce box white cake mix, plus ingredients called for on box

1 12-ounce can cream of coconut

1 14-ounce can sweetened condensed milk

1 8-ounce container nondairy whipped topping

1 cup shredded coconut

1. Bake cake according to the directions on the box. Meanwhile, thoroughly mix the cream of coconut and sweetened condensed milk.

2. Poke holes in cake at even intervals with a wooden skewer or a long-pronged fork. Pour coconut/condensed milk mixture over cake and let soak 8 hours.

3. Smooth whipped topping over cake and sprinkle with shredded coconut.


# Summer Celebration Berry Cake

*Nothing says summer like the taste of fresh berries. Bake some on the cake and serve some fresh as a garnish for a seasonal treat that's sure to please.*

**INGREDIENTS | SERVES 8**

3 eggs

¼ cup sugar

⅓ cup safflower oil

1 cup sour cream

Zest and juice of 2 lemons

1 18.25-ounce yellow cake mix with pudding

2 cups fresh, cleaned blueberries

Confectioners' sugar

1. Preheat oven to 350°F. Grease a bundt cake pan.

2. Beat eggs and sugar until light and frothy. Continue to beat and add oil, sour cream, lemon zest, and lemon juice. Mix until very smooth.

3. Fold in cake mix bit by bit. Mix until well blended. Add blueberries. Pour batter evenly into cake pan. Bake for 50 to 60 minutes. Top with confectioners' sugar.

# Pesach Banana Cake for Passover

*This recipe is used with permission from Torahwomen.com. It's one of their favorite Passover recipes.*

**INGREDIENTS | SERVES 6–8**

1 12-ounce box Manischewitz yellow cake mix

¼ cup water

2 eggs

1 cup mashed or puréed ripe bananas

⅓ cup semisweet chocolate chips

Kosher for Passover confectioners' sugar for garnish (optional)

Whipped cream (dairy meal) for garnish (optional)

Nondairy whipped topping (meat meal) for garnish (optional)

1. Preheat oven to 350°F. Spray an 8" or 9" square or round cake pan with nonstick cooking spray.

2. Beat together all ingredients except the chocolate chips and optional ingredients for 1–2 minutes until smooth.

3. Pour into prepared cake pan and sprinkle chocolate chips over top. Bake until cake springs back when gently pressed, about 25–35 minutes.

4. Remove from oven and leave cake in pan to cool for 15 minutes, then transfer to wire rack to cool completely.

5. Dust with confectioners' sugar if desired. Cut cake into slices. Serve each piece with a dollop of whipped cream or nondairy whipped topping if desired.

# Dulce de Leche Cream Cake

*This traditional cake is found in almost every Mexican bakery. Its milky
sweetness makes it a favorite for Cinco de Mayo celebrations.*

**INGREDIENTS | SERVES 8**

1 18.25-ounce box yellow cake mix plus ingredients called for on box

1 14-ounce can sweetened condensed milk

⅓ cup caramel ice cream topping

2 cups heavy whipping cream

1 teaspoon vanilla extract

¼ cup confectioners' sugar

⅓ cup sliced almonds, toasted

1. Bake cake in a square pan according to the cake mix instructions. Remove cake from oven and let cool for 5 minutes. Invert onto cooling rack and cool completely.

2. Meanwhile, pour condensed milk into a microwave-safe bowl and microwave for 2 minutes. Gently stir condensed milk.

3. Return to microwave and cook 2 more minutes on medium power. Continue to microwave in 5-minute intervals for 20 minutes, whisking gently between intervals.

4. When condensed milk is thick and the color of light caramel, stir in caramel topping. Let caramel mixture cool for 10 minutes. Frost cake with this mixture.

5. Beat whipping cream in a large mixing bowl until it forms soft peaks. Fold in vanilla and confectioners' sugar. Beat until stiff peaks form. Spoon whipped cream over cake.

6. Garnish with toasted almonds. Chill for 2 hours. Serve with rich coffee.

# Great Pumpkin Cake

*This structured cake makes a great holiday centerpiece and is sure
to be admired by ghost, goblins, and ghouls of all stripes!*

**INGREDIENTS | SERVES 9**

2 18.25-ounce boxes yellow cake plus
   ingredients called for on box

Orange food coloring

1 12-ounce tub white frosting

Fruit Roll-Up

1 Hostess Ho Ho

1. Prepare cake mixes according to cake mix instructions. Pour into 2 bundt cake pans and bake according to instructions. Invert cakes onto cooling rack. Mix orange food coloring into white frosting.

2. When cool, place one cake rounded side down onto a serving plate. Line upward edge of cake with orange frosting.

3. Place second bundt cake (right side up) on top of the first cake so that together they form a round, pumpkin-like shape.

4. Frost entire cake using up-and-down strokes. Cut Fruit Roll-Up into eye and mouth shapes. Lay shapes on cake to make a face.

5. Place Ho Ho in the round indentation in the top of the cake to look like a stem.

# Pumpkin Patch Cake

*The tastes of autumn star in this cake. For an extra-special treat,*
*pick the pumpkin yourself and create your own purée.*

**INGREDIENTS | SERVES 12**

1 18.25-ounce box spice cake mix
1 can pumpkin purée
1 cup mayonnaise
3 eggs
1 12-ounce tub cream cheese frosting

1. Preheat oven to 350°F. Grease cake pan.

2. Combine all ingredients. Turn batter into pan. Bake 35 minutes or until fork comes out clean. Cool completely. Frost with cream cheese frosting.

# Thanksgiving Pie Dump Cake

*This is a great recipe to pass family style or share at potluck dinners. It travels*
*well and is a warm, sweet, comforting dish that's sure to please.*

**INGREDIENTS | SERVES 12**

4 eggs
1 teaspoon cinnamon
1 cup sugar
1 14-ounce can pumpkin purée (not pie filling)
1 12-ounce can evaporated milk
1 18-ounce box yellow cake mix
1 cup butter
1 cup pecans
1 recipe Whipping Cream (page 166)

1. Preheat oven to 350°F. Grease a casserole dish.

2. Beat eggs, cinnamon, sugar, pumpkin, and evaporated milk in a large mixing bowl with a wooden spoon. Pour into casserole dish.

3. Layer dry yellow cake mix on top of pumpkin mixture. Dot with pats of butter. Garnish with pecans. Bake for 1 hour. When cool, top with whipping cream.

# Pecan Pie Casserole

*Pecan pie is a buttery, gooey, favorite cold-weather treat. Here you enjoy all the rich flavor of the pie, without needing to bake a crust from scratch. It's simple enough to make any weeknight, but yummy enough for holiday dinners.*

### INGREDIENTS | SERVES 12

1 18.25-ounce box yellow cake mix
4 eggs, divided use
½ cup butter, melted
1½ cups light corn syrup
½ cup dark brown sugar, packed
1 teaspoon vanilla
1½ cups chopped pecans

1. Preheat oven to 325°F. Grease a casserole dish.

2. Combine cake mix, 1 egg, and butter. Mix well. Set aside ½ cup of this mixture and pour remaining batter into casserole dish. Bake for 15 minutes.

3. Combine reserved batter, remaining 3 eggs, and the rest of ingredients in a bowl. Mix. Layer this mixture on top of baked layer and return to the oven for 50 minutes.

4. Cool and serve casserole style.

# Fresh from the Bog Cranberry Cobbler

*Thanksgiving is the perfect time to celebrate the tart, colorful cranberry. Paired with cherry filling, it offers a refreshingly tangy taste after a Thanksgiving feast.*

### INGREDIENTS | SERVES 12

1 18.25-ounce box white cake mix
1 teaspoon cinnamon
¼ teaspoon nutmeg
1 cup butter, softened
1 cup chopped walnuts (optional)
1 15-ounce can cherry pie filling
1 16-ounce can whole berry cranberry sauce
1 recipe Whipping Cream (page 166)

1. Preheat oven to 350°F.

2. Mix cake mix and spices in a large bowl. Crumble in butter. Sprinkle nuts into batter.

3. In a separate bowl, mix pie filling and cranberry sauce. Pour fruit mixture into casserole dish. Layer dry mixture over the top.

4. Bake for 50 minutes or until barely golden brown. Top generously with whipped cream.

# Cranberry Bundt Cake

*Sweet lemon zip and tangy cranberries blend together nicely in this creamy bundt cake.*
*Add a little orange flavoring, extract, or juice to the whipped topping*
*for a sweet citrus taste that complements cranberries beautifully.*

**INGREDIENTS | SERVES 15**

1 18.25-ounce box lemon cake mix
1 3-ounce package cream cheese
¾ cup milk
4 eggs
1¼ cups chopped cranberries
4 eggs
¼ cup sugar
Whipped topping

1. Preheat oven to 350°F. Grease a bundt pan.

2. In a large mixing bowl, combine cake mix, cream cheese, and milk. Beat for 2 minutes with an electric mixer.

3. In a separate bowl, combine cranberries and sugar. Add eggs. Fold berry mixture into batter. Pour into bundt pan. Bake for 55 minutes.

4. Serve slightly warm with a dollop of whipped topping.

# Cranberry Cream Cake

*Vanilla has been a favorite since ancient times. With extra vanilla flavor and crunchy whole*
*cranberries, this cake boasts a rich taste and texture worthy of your wildest daydreams.*

**INGREDIENTS | SERVES 12**

1 18.25-ounce box French vanilla cake mix
1 3.9-ounce box instant vanilla pudding
4 eggs
1 cup vanilla yogurt
¼ cup vegetable oil
1 8-ounce can whole berry cranberry sauce

1. Preheat oven to 350°F. Butter and flour a 9" × 13" pan.

2. Mix cake mix, pudding, eggs, yogurt, and oil in a large bowl. Beat for 2 minutes with an electric mixer. Spread more than half the batter in the pan.

3. Spoon cranberry sauce over batter in pan. Top with remaining batter. Bake for 45 minutes. Cool before serving.

# CHAPTER 13

## Local and Organic

# Organic Carrot Cake

*This wholesome, organic, less-sweet treat is a great choice for families looking to beat the sugar blues.*

**INGREDIENTS** | **SERVES 12**

1 18.25-ounce box organic carrot cake mix
1 cup organic carrots, grated
¼ cup organic applesauce
½ cup purified water

### Icing a Carrot Cake

Traditionally, carrot cakes are iced with sour cream frosting, but it's also lovely with a simple glaze. Use a fork to mix 4 tablespoons organic butter with ½ cup organic confectioners' sugar and 2 teaspoons organic vanilla extract. You'll have the cool sweetness of the icing without oversweetening the cake.

1. Preheat oven to 350°F. Butter a round 9" cake pan.

2. Scrub carrots with a vegetable brush but do not peel.

3. Mix cake mix, grated carrots, applesauce, and water in a large mixing bowl. Combine contents gently with a wooden mixing spoon until batter is moist.

4. Bake for 45 minutes.

# Turnip Spice Cake

*Warm, mashed turnips soothe the winter soul. Mashing turnips is easy. Simply scrub the turnips, cut into chunks, boil in water, and mash using a fork or ricer.*

**INGREDIENTS** | **SERVES 8**

1 18.25-ounce box spice cake mix plus ingredients called for on box
1 turnip, boiled, mashed, and cooled
1 cup raisins
4 tablespoons organic butter, melted
½ cup organic confectioners' sugar

1. Prepare and bake cake according to cake mix instructions, folding in mashed turnip and raisins after wet ingredients.

2. Allow cake to cool slightly. Whisk butter and confectioners' sugar together with a fork. Drizzle cake with glaze.

# Rhubarb Upside-Down Cake

*Rhubarb is best when accompanied by something sweet. Vanilla and butter fit the bill nicely. Feel like adding a little extra summer? Toss in a few ripe, sweet strawberries.*

**INGREDIENTS** | **SERVES 6**

3 tablespoons organic butter, melted

1 cup sugar

1 pound rhubarb, chopped

1 18.25-ounce box white cake mix plus ingredients called for on box

1. Preheat oven according to cake mix instructions. Butter an 8" square cake pan.

2. Combine melted butter and sugar and fold into chopped rhubarb. Transfer mixture to cake pan; spread evenly.

3. Mix batter according to cake mix instructions and pour over rhubarb mixture. Bake for 35 minutes.

4. Remove cake from oven and invert onto serving platter immediately. Spoon any remaining fruit or syrup remaining in pan onto top of cake.

# Easy Rhubarb Upside-Down Cake

*This recipe is from Leah Jewison, president of the Mankato Area Growers Association. She knows beautiful rhubarb when she sees it.*

**INGREDIENTS** | **SERVES 8**

1 cup brown sugar

3 cups rhubarb, chopped

1 18.25-ounce box yellow cake mix plus ingredients called for on box

1. Preheat oven according to cake mix instructions. Butter a 9" × 13" cake pan.

2. Sprinkle brown sugar across the bottom of the pan. Layer chopped rhubarb on top of brown sugar.

3. Prepare batter according to cake mix instructions. Pour over rhubarb. Bake according to instructions. Allow cake to cool, then invert onto serving platter.

# Strawberry-Rhubarb Crumble

*Strawberries and rhubarb are the taste of summer. If you've never cooked with rhubarb before, give it a try. It has a reddish color and is sold in long stalks.*

**INGREDIENTS | SERVES 8**

1½ cups fresh rhubarb, cut into 1" pieces

1 quart fresh strawberries, hulled and quartered

Juice of 1 lemon

½ cup sugar

½ cup flour

Pinch salt

1 18.25-ounce box white cake mix

½ cup organic butter

Whipped cream, fresh cream, or ice cream to garnish (optional)

1. Preheat oven to 375°F.

2. Combine rhubarb, strawberries, lemon juice, sugar, flour, and salt in a casserole dish and mix gently but completely with a wooden spoon.

3. Layer cake mix over fruit.

4. Cut butter into pats and use to dot the top layer evenly.

5. Bake for 45 minutes, or until fruit bubbles up and top layer is golden.

6. Garnish with whipped cream, fresh cream, or ice cream if desired.

## Rhubarb Tea

You can make your own lovely rhubarb tea. Simply juice the rhubarb stalks, strain the juice through cheesecloth, and strain off any froth. Mix 2 cups rhubarb juice with 6 cups water, and sweeten with 2 cups sugar. Serve over ice and garnish with fresh mint.

# Sauerkraut Black Forest Cake

*If you're lucky enough to have a vendor who sells homemade sauerkraut at
your local farmers' market, use some of it to try this tasty treat!*

**INGREDIENTS | SERVES 12**

1 18.25-ounce package devil's food cake
  mix

⅔ cup water

3 eggs

½ cup vegetable oil

1 cup sauerkraut

1 15-ounce can cherry pie filling

1 recipe Whipping Cream for garnish
  (page 166)

1. Preheat oven to 350°F. Grease and flour cake pans. Set aside.

2. Beat cake mix, water, eggs, and oil in a large mixing bowl, using an electric mixer set to high speed until all ingredients are completely incorporated. Gently fold in sauerkraut.

3. Turn batter into pans and bake for 30 minutes or until the center of the cake bounces back when touched gently.

4. Allow cake to cool for 15 minutes in the pan before turning out onto a wire rack.

5. Top with cherry pie filling and a dollop of whipped topping.

# Chocolate Beet Cake

*Fresh beets are irresistibly beautiful when you see them at the farmers' market. The challenge comes when cooking them at home. Don't let them languish in the crisper—pop them in a cake.*

**INGREDIENTS | SERVES 8**

1 18-ounce package chocolate cake mix plus ingredients called for on box

3 cups organic beets, shredded

4 tablespoons organic butter, melted

½ cup organic confectioners' sugar

## About Beets

Beets are high in vitamins A and C and well worth using. To prepare, simply scrub beets with a vegetable scrubber and shred with a grater or food processor. (Skip peeling to benefit from the trace minerals that live near the surface of the vegetable.) Remember, beet juice stains. Wear gloves and work with steel utensils whenever possible.

1. Prepare and bake cake according to cake mix instructions, folding beets in as you add wet ingredients.

2. Allow cake to cool slightly. Whisk butter and confectioners' sugar together with a fork. Drizzle cake with glaze.

# Pumpkin Bread

*Whether the pumpkin is from the patch or from a can, it adds wholesome nutrition and sweet, moist flavor to a cake.*

**INGREDIENTS | SERVES 8**

1 18.25-ounce box yellow cake mix
2 cups Baking Pumpkin (page 212)
½ cup organic molasses
4 eggs
1 teaspoon cinnamon
1 teaspoon ground nutmeg
1 cup chopped pecans (optional)
⅓ cup dried cranberries or raisins

1. Preheat oven to 350°F. Grease two 9½" loaf pans.

2. Combine all ingredients in a large mixing bowl and mix well with an electric mixer set to medium speed. Divide mixture evenly between the pans and bake for 1 hour.

3. Allow to cool before turning out of pans.

## Buying Pumpkin

Look for pie pumpkins or other small pumpkins with thicker walls when you're choosing one for baking. Most jack-o'-lantern pumpkins are bred for other uses. Do not bake your jack-o'-lantern if it is more than one day old; it may not be safe.

# Baking Pumpkin

*Baking with pumpkin is easier than you might think. Simply divide this recipe's yield into batches of 2 cups (equivalent to the amount found in a can) and freeze in resealable plastic bags until ready to bake.*

**INGREDIENTS | YIELDS 4 CUPS**

Pumpkin

Water

### Oven-Baked Pumpkin

If you don't have a steamer, you can halve the pumpkin and bake it in the oven. Simply place it cut-side down in a pan filled with 1" water. Bake at 350°F for 50 minutes and proceed with Step 2.

1. Wash pumpkin and cut in half. Place 1 pumpkin half in a steamer; if it is too big, cut to fit. Steam each half for 20 minutes or until tender.

2. Allow pumpkin to cool before peeling off rind or scooping out flesh.

3. Purée pumpkin flesh and strain out excess water through a cheesecloth-lined strainer.

# Spicy Squash Cake

*Prepare the squash as you would the Baking Pumpkin (page 212).*

**INGREDIENTS | SERVES 12**

1 18-ounce box spice cake mix plus ingredients called for on box (except water)

2 cups butternut squash, cooked and mashed

1 12-ounce tub prepared cream cheese frosting

1. Prepare batter according to cake mix instructions, substituting squash for water. Add a touch of water if batter appears too dry. Bake according to instructions.

2. Allow cake to cool before frosting.

# Fresh Berry Lemon Cake

*Share this cake with friends each year to celebrate the first harvest of berries from the backyard. Keep the recipe special by making it a once-a-year ritual.*

**INGREDIENTS | SERVES 8**

1 18.25-ounce box lemon cake mix

1 teaspoon baking powder

1 cup fresh berries

1 cup sour cream

4 eggs

1 tablespoon oil

Lemon zest to taste

Additional berries and whipped cream (optional)

1. Preheat oven to 350°F. Grease and flour a bundt pan.

2. Combine cake mix and baking powder in a large mixing bowl. In a separate bowl, mix berries, sour cream, eggs, oil, and lemon zest. Fold dry ingredients into wet.

3. Turn batter into the bundt pan and bake for 45 minutes. Allow cake to cool slightly before turning onto rack or serving plate.

4. Serve with fresh berries and whipped cream if desired.

# Harvest Squash Cobbler

*Butternut squash is a versatile vegetable. It's beautiful steamed or puréed and it's just as lovely baked in a beautiful spice cake. Spice and ginger add zip to this dessert.*

**INGREDIENTS | SERVES 8**

1 large butternut squash
2 cups sugar
2 teaspoons cinnamon
2 teaspoons pumpkin pie seasoning
1 teaspoon ground ginger
1 12-ounce can evaporated milk
4 eggs
1 18.25-ounce box yellow cake mix
1 cup organic butter, melted
Whipped topping for garnish

1. Preheat oven to 350°F.

2. Halve the butternut squash. Clean out the seeds and microwave squash for 10 minutes. Peel and cut squash into 1" cubes. Place in a 9" × 13" pan.

3. Combine sugar, spices, evaporated milk, and eggs and pour over the squash. Crumble dry cake mix over both these layers and top liberally with melted butter.

4. Bake for 45 minutes. Serve warm with a dollop of whipped topping.

## Add-Ins and Variations

Keep your favorite recipes fresh and exciting by adding a little something unexpected now and then. Pecans, brown sugar, and dried fruit are fun add-ins. Try them or anything else you have on hand.

# Sunshine State Cake

*If you're lucky enough to have fresh organic oranges growing near you, pick them and get baking. Whether they're straight from the yard or the market, citrus is a beautiful choice for dessert.*

**INGREDIENTS | SERVES 8**

2 eggs

1 18.25-ounce box yellow cake mix

1 3.9-ounce package instant yellow pudding mix

¾ cup water

½ cup cooking oil

⅓ cup fresh-squeezed orange juice

2 cups confectioners' sugar

3 oranges for garnish

1. Preheat oven to 350°F. Grease and flour a tube pan.

2. In a mixing bowl, beat eggs, cake mix, pudding mix, water, and oil with an electric mixer and turn into the pan. Bake for 50 minutes.

3. Allow cake to cool completely in pan.

4. As cake cools, make a glaze by boiling orange juice and sugar in a small saucepan, stirring in fresh orange zest to taste.

5. When cake is completely cool, remove it to a serving platter, drizzle with glaze, and garnish with fresh orange slices.

# Juiciest Poke Cake

*Consider using more than one juice to form your glaze. Try adding a dash of pomegranate or strawberry for a colorful burst of flavor.*

**INGREDIENTS | SERVES 8**

1 18.25-ounce box orange-flavored cake mix plus ingredients called for on box

2 cups confectioners' sugar

⅓ cup fresh-squeezed citrus juice

2 tablespoons butter, melted

1 tablespoon butter

Citrus zest

Citrus fruit for garnish

1. Prepare and bake cake according to package instructions. Poke holes in the cake with a clean skewer. Combine sugar, juice, butter, and water to form a glaze.

2. Pour glaze over cake and allow cake to cool completely. Garnish with zest and sections of fruit.

# A Is for Apple Cake

*Got a field trip to the orchard planned? Bake this cake when you get back as you talk over your favorite memories of the day. Try Piñata, Braeburn, or Gala apples for baking.*

**INGREDIENTS | SERVES 8**

½ cup chopped walnuts

1 18.25-ounce box spice cake mix

1 3.9-ounce box butterscotch instant pudding mix

4 eggs

½ cup vegetable oil

½ cup cold water

3 medium fresh organic apples, cored, peeled, and chopped

1 cup dried cranberries

Confectioners' sugar for garnish

1. Preheat oven to 325°F. Butter a tube pan and sprinkle the bottom with chopped walnuts.

2. Combine cake mix, pudding, eggs, oil, and water in a large mixing bowl using an electric mixer set to medium speed.

3. Gently fold in apples and dried cranberries so they are distributed evenly throughout the batter. Pour into pan and bake for 55 minutes.

4. Invert cake onto wire rack to cool. Sprinkle with confectioners' sugar.

# Ginny Sawyer's Freezer Preserves

*Making preserves is an easy family project that will provide sweet delights all the year through. Serve for dessert and again on warm toast with a thick layer of butter.*

**INGREDIENTS** | **MAKES 7½ PINTS**

3 cups berries

5 cups sugar

5 tablespoons pectin

1 cup water

1. Wash, stem, and crush berries. Mix with sugar and let stand 30 minutes.

2. Mix pectin and water; bring to a boil and boil for 1 minute. Stir into berry mixture. Stir with a wooden spoon for 2 minutes.

3. Put in freezer-safe containers, leaving ½ inch air at the top. Let stand 24 hours to set, and then freeze. Thaw when ready to serve.

# Farmers' Market Trifle

*Have an overabundance of fresh fruit? What a wonderful dilemma! This recipe is one of many creative ways you'll find to celebrate and enjoy the taste of summer.*

**INGREDIENTS | SERVES 6–8**

1 18.25-ounce box organic angel food cake mix plus ingredients called for on box

½ cup organic milk

½ cup organic vanilla yogurt

1 3.9-ounce box organic instant pudding mix

4 cups peaches or other juicy fresh fruit

Fresh whipped cream

## Get Your Fruit Ready

There's much more to storing fruit than stashing it in the fridge. Most fruits will turn grainy and wilt if they get much cooler than 30°F. Citrus fruit has an even lower tolerance level for cold temperatures. Many fruits will do just fine—and even continue to ripen—outside the fridge. If you're just waiting a day or two to eat them, consider displaying fruit in a bowl in the kitchen.

1. Prepare and bake angel food cake according to cake mix instructions.

2. As cake bakes, combine milk, yogurt, and pudding mix in a large bowl using an electric mixer set to high speed. Let stand 10 minutes.

3. When cake is baked and cooled, cut into bite-sized cubes.

4. Place a layer of cake cubes in the bottom of a large glass bowl, follow with a layer of fresh fruit, and top with milk mixture. Repeat until bowl is nearly full.

5. Top with whipped cream. Keep cool until ready to serve.

# Organic Grasshopper Brownies

*A healthier take on an indulgent favorite, this is an ideal choice to satisfy your sweet tooth without abandoning your commitment to eating organic.*

**INGREDIENTS | SERVES 12**

1 10-ounce box organic chocolate biscotti mix

2 large eggs

5 tablespoons organic butter, melted

Organic chocolate morsels

3 tablespoons organic peppermint flavor

## Shopping Organic

Finding organic ingredients has never been easier. Organic mixes are readily available online as well as in co-ops and at grocers everywhere. You often pay a premium and you might have to go a little out of your way for these ingredients, but the taste and purity are worth it!

1. Preheat oven to 350°F. Grease and flour 8" × 8" cake pan. Set aside.

2. In a large mixing bowl, combine biscotti mix, eggs, butter, chocolate morsels, and peppermint flavor.

3. Use an electric mixer set to medium speed to combine ingredients. Pour batter into pan. Bake for 25 minutes.

# Fruit Stand Jam Cake

*This lovely dessert is one of the many simple ways to enjoy the taste of beautifully fresh fruit. With only two ingredients, it's easy to bake up any time you've got a hankering.*

**INGREDIENTS | SERVES 15**

1 18.25-ounce box white cake mix marked "just add water"

1 12-ounce jar freezer preserves

1. Preheat oven to 350°F. Grease a bundt pan.

2. Combine preserves and cake mix in a large mixing bowl. Mix using a wooden spoon; do not expect a smooth batter. Pour into pan. Bake for 25 minutes.

# Zucchini Cake

*Zucchini is a delicate squash that is in season during mid- and late summer in most climates. Try to use fresh zucchini immediately and avoid refrigerating if possible. Zucchini hates the cold!*

**INGREDIENTS** | **SERVES 8**

1 18.25-ounce box devil's food cake mix
1 teaspoon ground cinnamon
3 eggs
1¼ cups apple juice
1 cup organic zucchini, shredded
4-ounce cream cheese, softened
2 teaspoons lemon juice
Zucchini peel

1. Preheat oven to 350°F. Flour and grease a 10" tube pan.

2. Combine cake mix, ground cinnamon, and eggs and beat for 2 minutes. Shred zucchini using a large-holed grater or a food processor. Fold zucchini in gently.

3. Turn batter into pan and spread evenly. Bake for 55 minutes.

4. Allow cake to cool. Mix softened cream cheese and lemon juice for frosting. Frost cake and garnish lightly with zucchini zest.

# Smoothie Splash Pound Cake

*Need a little boost of antioxidants or vitamin C on a cold night? Bake a pound cake with a hidden punch!*

**INGREDIENTS | SERVES 12**

1 16-ounce box organic pound cake mix
¾ cup organic smoothie
2 eggs
3 lemons
2 limes
¼ cup packed brown sugar

1. Preheat oven to 350°F. Grease a loaf pan.

2. Mix cake mix, smoothie, and eggs according to cake mix instructions. Bake according to package directions.

3. Allow cake to cool in the pan on a wire rack for 15 minutes before turning onto a serving platter. Juice lemons and limes and stir in brown sugar to make glaze. Use to top the cake.

# CHAPTER 14

# Vegetarian Cakes

# DIY Vegan Cake Mix

*A great way to ensure wholesome and vegan cake is to add all the ingredients yourself. On a rainy day, make up a few batches of cake mix and enjoy simple baking later.*

**INGREDIENTS** | **MAKES 5 CUPS**

3 cups flour
2 cups sugar
8 tablespoons cocoa
2 teaspoons baking soda
2 teaspoons salt

1. Combine all ingredients. Stir to mix. Store in an airtight container.

2. To bake cake, preheat oven to 375°F. Combine mix, 2 cups water, 1½ teaspoons vanilla, 2 tablespoons vinegar, and ¾ cup canola oil. Bake for 30 minutes.

## Converting Recipes

Cooking vegan doesn't always mean abandoning all your favorite old recipes. In some cases you'll be able to replace dairy milk with soy milk, butter with margarine, and eggs with Ener-G Egg Replacer or banana.

# Super Quick Vegan Cookies

*Vegan treats don't have to take tons of time and a lengthy list of ingredients. There are great shortcuts; this recipe is one of them.*

**INGREDIENTS** | **MAKES 24 COOKIES**

1 18.25-ounce box vegan cake mix
1 cup unsalted vegan margarine
3 teaspoons Ener-G Egg Replacer
4 tablespoons warm water
1½ cups vegan chocolate chips (optional)

1. Mix all ingredients in a bowl. Chill at least 1 hour or overnight.

2. Preheat oven to 350°F.

3. Drop batter onto nonstick cookie sheet in small balls. Bake for 12 minutes or until golden brown. Remove from sheet and place on cooling rack.

# Vegan Pumpkin Cookies

*This classic vegan treat for autumn days goes great with a steaming mug of coffee.*

**INGREDIENTS | MAKES 24 COOKIES**

2 boxes spice cake mix
1 29-ounce can organic pumpkin purée
2 cups vegan chocolate chips (optional)

1. Preheat oven to 350°F.

2. Mix all ingredients thoroughly. Drop by spoonfuls onto a nonstick cookie sheet. Bake for 10–12 minutes. Cool on a rack.

# Vegan Yellow Cake Sugar Cookies

*This is a great base for iced holiday cookies or cutouts.*

**INGREDIENTS | MAKES 24 COOKIES**

1 18-ounce box vegan yellow cake mix
3 teaspoons Ener-G Egg Replacer
4 tablespoons warm water
¼ cup oil
½ cup brown sugar

1. Preheat oven to 350°F.

2. Mix all ingredients well. Gather up dough and roll out on a well-floured surface. Cut with a biscuit cutter or the top edge of a drinking glass.

3. Transfer with spatula to nonstick cookie sheet. Bake for 8–10 minutes or until golden. Cool.

# Famous Vegan Fizz Cake

*Ask a vegan for a cake mix recipe and you'll undoubtedly hear about the simple soda cake.*
*This amazing recipe calls for only two ingredients and is very easy to bake.*
*It's a great go-to staple any time you need a vegan treat.*

**INGREDIENTS** | **SERVES 12**

1 18-ounce box vegan cake mix
1¼ cups non-diet soda

1. Preheat oven according to cake mix instructions. Lightly grease cake pan or bundt pan with vegan margarine or a vegan spray.

2. Gently stir together cake mix and soda. Do not overstir; you want to preserve the soda's fizz. Pour mixture into pan.

3. Bake according to cake mix instructions.

# Vegan Chocolate Fizz Bundt Cake

*Whip up the taste of an old-fashioned chocolate cola for a truly decadent desert. This is a convenient vegan treat that's easy to keep on hand to satisfy cravings for something sweet.*

**INGREDIENTS** | **SERVES 12**

1 18.25-ounce box chocolate cake mix
1 12-ounce can cola
Vegan Bundt Cake Glaze (page 227)

1. Preheat oven according to cake mix instructions. Lightly grease cake pan or bundt pan with vegan margarine or a vegan spray.

2. Gently stir together cake mix and soda. Do not overstir; you want to preserve the soda's fizz. Pour mixture into pan.

3. Bake according to cake mix instructions. Cool and frost with Vegan Bundt Cake Glaze.

# Vegan Bundt Cake Glaze

*A milk-free chocolate glaze adds a bit of super-sweetness to your vegan bundt cake. Easy to make and fun to drizzle, there's no reason not to try this wonder recipe.*

**INGREDIENTS | SERVES 12**

¼ cup melted vegan chocolate chips
¾ cup rice milk

Mix melted chocolate chips and rice milk together. Drizzle over cake.

# Vegan Cherry Cola Cake

*Committing to a vegan diet doesn't mean giving up all your favorite fast foods. Here's a way to satisfy a soda craving without downing a whole can.*

**INGREDIENTS | SERVES 12**

1 18-ounce box chocolate cake mix
1 12-ounce can cherry cola
Vegan Bundt Cake Glaze (above)

1. Preheat oven according to cake mix instructions. Lightly grease cake pan or bundt pan with vegan margarine or a vegan spray.

2. Gently stir together cake mix and soda. Do not overstir; you want to preserve the soda's fizz. Pour mixture into pan.

3. Bake according to cake mix instructions. Cool and frost with Vegan Bundt Cake Glaze.

# Vegan Spice Cake

*Simple fizz cake gets a little fancy in this still-simple recipe. Four ingredients are all it takes to bake up a beautiful cake.*

**INGREDIENTS | SERVES 12**

1 18-ounce box chocolate cake mix
1 12-ounce can Dr. Pepper
2 cups raisins
Vegan Bundt Cake Glaze (page 227)

1. Preheat oven according to cake mix instructions. Lightly grease cake pan or bundt pan with vegan margarine or a vegan spray.

2. Gently stir together cake mix and soda. Do not overstir; you want to preserve the soda's fizz. Stir in raisins. Pour mixture into pan.

3. Bake according to cake mix instructions. Frost with Vegan Bundt Cake Glaze.

# Fancy Red Fizz Cake

*For anyone with egg, nut, or dairy allergies, this recipe is a lifesaver. This simple cake is bright, cheery, pleasing, and safe for those who need to steer clear of allergens. Just to be on the safe side, be sure to double-check for allergens in the ingredients listed on the cake mix box.*

**INGREDIENTS | SERVES 12**

9.9-ounce box allergen-free white cake mix
2 tablespoons unsweetened cocoa
1 12-ounce can ginger ale or other clear soda
2 teaspoons vanilla extract
Red food coloring
1 12-ounce tub cream cheese or chocolate frosting

1. Preheat oven according to cake mix instructions.

2. Sift cake mix and cocoa in a bowl. Add soda and beat with an electric mixer. Add vanilla. Add food coloring.

3. Pour into a pan and bake according to cake mix instructions. Frost with cream cheese or chocolate icing.

# Chocolate Pumpkin Muffins

*This quick and easy recipe is good to try for people who have
food allergies, or for groups of young children.*

### INGREDIENTS | SERVES 24

1 29-ounce can organic pumpkin purée
1 16.4-ounce box dairy- and egg-free
   organic chocolate cake mix

1. Preheat oven according to cake mix instructions. Line muffin tins with paper baking cups.

2. Blend pumpkin purée into cake mix. Pour into muffin tins. Bake according to cake mix instructions for muffins.

# Vegan Vanilla Icing

*This vegan royal icing is perfect for fancy wedding and birthday cakes, so
you can celebrate in style and stay true to your vegan lifestyle.*

### INGREDIENTS | MAKES 4 CUPS

2 cups Crisco
1 cup icing sugar
½ cup water
1 tablespoon vanilla

Combine all ingredients with electric mixer on low speed for 1 minute. Scrape sides of bowl. Mix for another minute.

# Vegan Chocolate Frosting

*The creamy, buttery taste of this rich, fudgy frosting will fool people into thinking it's not really vegan.*

### INGREDIENTS | 8 CUPS

1 cup vegan margarine
1 cup unsweetened cocoa powder
5⅓ cups confectioners' sugar
½ cup water
2 teaspoons vanilla

1. Mix vegan margarine and cocoa powder with electric mixer set to low speed. Slowly introduce confectioners' sugar and water, alternating between the two.

2. Mix at a slightly higher speed until desired consistency is achieved. Add vanilla.


# Vegan Dump Cake

*Dump cake is a favorite potluck treat, and now it's been modified to serve to your vegan friends too! Using this recipe as a template, you can veganize other dump cake recipes in this book.*

### INGREDIENTS | SERVES 12

1 can crushed pineapple
1 can blueberry pie filling
1 18.5-ounce box Duncan Hines yellow cake mix
½ cup vegan margarine
1 tablespoon brown sugar

1. Preheat oven according to cake mix instructions. Grease a pan.

2. Pour pineapple into prepared pan. Layer in blueberry pie filling. Top with cake mix. Dot with chunks of margarine. Bake according to cake mix instructions. Allow to cool. Sprinkle with brown sugar.

# Vegan Applesauce Cake

*This dish is easy to bake, simple to serve, and easy to transport. Take it along and watch it disappear.*

**INGREDIENTS | SERVES 12**

1 tablespoon flour
1 18.5-ounce box Duncan Hines yellow cake mix
⅓ cup organic applesauce
3 bananas, mashed
1¼ cups water

1. Preheat oven to 350°F.

2. Add flour to cake mix and sift. Add applesauce and bananas. Stir in water. Pour into nonstick pan. Bake according to package directions.

# Sugar Cake

*Combine gooey brown sugar and light yellow cake for this lovely, versatile dessert. Serve with sliced peaches or other fleshy fruits for an extra luscious treat.*

**INGREDIENTS | SERVES 8**

½ cup soy margarine
½ cup brown sugar
½ cup soy milk
1 18.5-ounce box Duncan Hines yellow cake
Sugar Cake Topping (page 232)

1. Preheat oven to 350°F. Lightly grease a sheet cake pan.

2. Melt margarine in saucepan over low heat. Whisk in brown sugar and soy milk. Remove from heat. Pour into sheet cake pan.

3. Layer cake mix on top of the brown sugar mixture. Shake pan to even out mixture. Bake for 10 minutes. Remove from pan. Cool on rack.

4. Frost with Sugar Cake Topping.

# Sugar Cake Topping

*With only two ingredients to keep on hand, this frosting can be
ready to go in a snap any time the urge to bake strikes.*

**INGREDIENTS | SERVES 8**

1 3-ounce package instant vanilla
pudding
1 16-ounce tub nondairy whipped
topping

Mix pudding and nondairy whipped topping gently.
Spread onto cake. Keep cake cool until ready to serve.

# Vegan Brownie Bites

*Sometimes a tiny bite of sweetness is just enough to satisfy your
sweet tooth. These are great for lunches or snacks.*

**INGREDIENTS | SERVES 24**

1 18.25-ounce box vegan chocolate cake
mix
1 29-ounce can organic pumpkin purée
2 cups vegan chocolate morsels
1 cup chopped walnuts

1. Preheat oven to 350°F.

2. Use an electric mixer to combine cake mix and
   pumpkin until completely incorporated. Fold in
   chocolate morsels and walnuts.

3. Drop by spoonfuls onto nonstick baking sheet. Bake
   for 10 minutes. Cool on a wire rack.

# Eggless Yellow Cake

*This is the perfect recipe for vegetarians who are okay with milk but want to avoid eggs. This basic yellow cake recipe is a perfect canvas for your creative touch. Consider adding chocolate chips, butterscotch pieces, candies, or fresh fruit to this recipe.*

**INGREDIENTS | SERVES 12**

1 3-ounce box vanilla pudding (not instant)

2 cups milk

1 18.5-ounce box Duncan Hines yellow cake mix

1 12-ounce tub prepared frosting

1. Preheat oven to 350°F. Butter and flour a 13" × 9" × 2" baking pan. Set aside.

2. Mix pudding and milk.

3. In a large mixing bowl combine pudding and dry cake mix. Use an electric mixer to blend until batter is completely smooth.

4. Pour into pan and bake for 25 minutes. Allow cake to cool completely before frosting.

# Vegan Strawberry Shortcake

*Bake up this not-too-sweet treat on a beautiful summer day. For a lighter, spongier cake, substitute yellow cake mix for Bisquick. For a richer, thicker dessert, substitute Vegan Brownie Bites (page 232) for biscuits.*

**INGREDIENTS | SERVES 4**

4 sliced strawberries

½ cup sugar

2¼ cups Bisquick

⅔ cup soy milk

½ cup vegan margarine

Vegan whipped topping

1. Preheat oven to 450°F.

2. Mix sliced strawberries with sugar in a large mixing bowl. Set aside. In a separate bowl, mix Bisquick, soy milk, and margarine until a smooth dough forms.

3. Drop by spoonfuls onto nonstick cookie sheet. Bake 9 minutes or until slightly golden.

4. Remove from oven and let biscuits cool thoroughly before topping with strawberries and whipped topping.

# CHAPTER 15

# Special Diets and Allergies

# Basic DIY Cake Mix

*Want to enjoy the convenience of baking with a mix but need to keep an eye out for allergens and other problematic ingredients? Make your own cake mix. This mix will keep three weeks in the refrigerator and three months in the freezer.*

**INGREDIENTS | MAKES 12 CUPS**

7½ cups sifted flour

1 tablespoon salt

4½ cups sugar

4 tablespoons double-acting baking powder

¾ cup unsalted butter

1. Combine all ingredients except butter in a large mixing bowl and mix well.

2. Cut butter into fine pats and run through a food processor with 2½ cups of the flour mixture. Stop when the mixture is quite fine.

3. Combine processed mixture with remaining flour mixture. Mix thoroughly. Place 4 cups mixture in each of 3 resealable plastic bags for future use.

4. Label and refrigerate or freeze mixture until ready to use.

# Yellow Cake from DIY Mix

*Yellow cake is a staple of many of the recipes in this book. This basic cake will taste similar to yellow cakes made from mixes but will not include dyes, preservatives, and other ingredients that can spark allergic reactions.*

**INGREDIENTS | SERVES 8–12**

4 cups Basic DIY Cake Mix (above)

1 cup skim milk

2 teaspoons vanilla

¼ cup unsalted butter, softened

3 eggs

1. Preheat oven to 350°F. Grease and flour cake pans. Set aside.

2. Pour cake mix into a large bowl. Make a well in the center. Add skim milk, vanilla, and butter. Beat for 3 minutes or until a smooth batter forms. Add eggs and thoroughly combine. Pour into pans.

3. Bake for 35 minutes or until the center of the cake springs back when lightly touched.

# White Cake from DIY Mix

*This recipe for white cake provides a beautiful base for frosted birthday and wedding cakes. It's simpler than baking from scratch, but you can control your own ingredients.*

**INGREDIENTS | SERVES 8–12**

4 cups Basic DIY Cake Mix (page 236)
1 cup skim milk
2 teaspoons vanilla
¼ cup unsalted butter, softened
3 egg whites

1. Preheat oven to 350°F. Grease and flour cake pans. Set aside.

2. Pour cake mix into a large bowl. Make a well in the center. Add skim milk, vanilla, and butter. Beat for 3 minutes or until a smooth batter forms. Add egg whites and thoroughly combine. Pour into a pan.

3. Bake for 35 minutes or until the center of the cake springs back when lightly touched.

# Spice Cake from DIY Mix

*Create your own warm, spicy, nourishing cakes with this spectacular combination. Add a little more of your favorite flavors for a blend that's all your own.*

**INGREDIENTS | SERVES 8–12**

4 cups Basic DIY Cake Mix (page 236)
1 teaspoon freshly ground cinnamon
½ teaspoon ground allspice
¼ teaspoon ground cloves
1 cup skim milk
2 teaspoons vanilla
¼ cup unsalted butter, softened
3 eggs

1. Preheat oven to 350°F. Grease and flour cake pans. Set aside.

2. Mix cake mix and spices in a large bowl. Make a well in the center. Add milk, vanilla, and butter. Beat for 3 minutes or until a smooth batter forms. Add eggs and thoroughly combine. Pour into a pan.

3. Bake for 35 minutes or until the center of the cake springs back when lightly touched.

# Strawberry Cake from DIY Mix

*This simple strawberry cake contains sugar and spice and everything nice, so it's perfect for a girly cake—but the boys like the taste, too!*

**INGREDIENTS | SERVES 8–12**

4 cups Basic DIY Cake Mix (page 236)
2 teaspoons vanilla
3 egg whites
1 cup skim milk
1 10-ounce package frozen strawberries, thawed
¼ cup softened, unsalted butter

1. Preheat oven to 350°F. Grease and flour cake pans. Set aside.

2. Pour cake mix into a large bowl. Make a well in the center. Add skim milk, strawberries, and butter. Beat for 3 minutes or until a smooth batter forms. Add vanilla and egg whites; thoroughly combine. Pour into cake pans.

3. Bake for 35 minutes or until the center of the cake springs back when lightly touched.

# "Flour" to Make Gluten-Free DIY Cake Mix

*Substitute this mixture for flour in the DIY Cake Mix recipes to create gluten-free cake mixes. It is easier than ever to find gluten-free baking mixes and baked goods, but it's just as easy to create your own mixes and use them to try other recipes in this book.*

**INGREDIENTS | 6 CUPS**

3 cups finely ground brown rice flour
1 cup potato starch
½ cup tapioca flour
1¼ teaspoons xanthan or guar gum

Sift all ingredients together and blend thoroughly. Substitute for flour in DIY cake mix recipes.

# Dye- and Milk-Free Chocolate Frosting

*This recipe is free of milk, dye, nuts, and other common allergens.*
*It's a yummy and safe bet for food-sensitive folks.*

**INGREDIENTS | 4 CUPS**

½ cup allergy-safe margarine, softened
½ cup unsweetened cocoa
2⅔ cups confectioners' sugar
¼ cup water
1 teaspoon pure organic vanilla extract

Beat margarine using an electric mixer set to low speed. Add other ingredients and mix until completely incorporated. Use to top a cooled cake.

# No-Dye Red Velvet Cake

*Love red velvet cake but worried about food coloring allergies? Here's*
*a naturally sweet solution rich in color, texture, and flavor.*

**INGREDIENTS | SERVES 8**

1 18.25-ounce box white cake mix plus ingredients called for on box
1 cup canned puréed cooked beets
1 teaspoon vanilla extract
1 12-ounce tub prepared cream cheese frosting

1. Preheat oven according to cake mix instructions.

2. Mix batter according to instructions, adding in beets and vanilla before mixing batter. Bake according to instructions. Allow to cool completely. Frost.

# Chocolate Cake from DIY Mix

*Finally, easy-to-bake chocolate cake without all the colors and artificial flavors! Starting with DIY Mix makes it easy. Selecting your own ingredients makes it wholesome.*

**INGREDIENTS | SERVES 8–12**

4 cups Basic DIY Cake Mix (page 236)

1 cup plus 2 tablespoons skim milk, divided

2 teaspoons vanilla

¼ cup unsalted butter, softened

3 eggs

2 squares unsweetened chocolate, melted

3 tablespoons cocoa powder

1. Preheat oven to 350°F. Grease and flour cake pans. Set aside.

2. Pour cake mix into a large bowl. Make a well in the center. Add 1 cup skim milk, vanilla, and butter. Beat for 3 minutes or until a smooth batter forms.

3. Add remaining 2 tablespoons skim milk, melted chocolate, and cocoa powder. Beat using an electric mixer until batter and chocolate are fully incorporated. Add eggs and thoroughly combine. Pour batter into cake pans.

4. Bake for 35 minutes or until the center of the cake springs back when lightly touched.

# Cherrybrook Kitchen's Chocolate Cake
# with Raspberry Filling

*This is a fruity, chocolaty recipe that's egg and dairy free. It's safe for many diets and delicious too.*

**INGREDIENTS | SERVES 8**

2 boxes Cherrybrook Kitchen Chocolate Cake mix and ingredients called for on box

1 box Cherrybrook Kitchen Chocolate Frosting mix and ingredients called for on box

½ cup seedless raspberry preserves

½ pint fresh raspberries

1. Prepare and bake cake according to package instructions for two layer cakes. Set cake aside to cool.

2. While cake is cooling, prepare chocolate frosting according to package instructions. Set aside.

3. Place one cake on a serving platter and spread with a thin layer of frosting.

4. Top with raspberry jam, leaving a ½" border around the edge to ensure that jam doesn't run over the sides.

5. Place second cake round on top of the first and frost top and sides with remaining frosting. Arrange berries as desired on top of cake.

6. Chill cake until ready to serve.

# Gluten-Free Vanilla Cake

*Baking can be the trickiest part of observing a gluten-free diet. Gluten-free mixes make it easy, delicious, and almost foolproof.*

### INGREDIENTS | SERVES 6

1 15-ounce box Gluten-Free Pantry Old Fashioned cake mix

1 3.9-ounce box instant vanilla pudding

½ cup sugar

5 eggs

½ cup olive oil

¾ cup orange or cranberry juice

1½ teaspoons vanilla extract

1. Preheat oven to 350°F. Flour and grease cake pan. Set aside.

2. Combine cake mix, pudding mix, and sugar in a medium bowl. In a separate bowl, combine eggs, olive oil, juice, and vanilla extract in a mixing bowl and combine thoroughly using an electric mixer set to high speed. Add dry ingredients and thoroughly incorporate. Turn batter into prepared cake pan.

3. Bake for 45 minutes, or until a toothpick comes out clean. Allow cake to cool completely before frosting.

### Where to Find Gluten-Free Mixes

If you have a health food store nearby, you have a go-to spot for gluten-free mixes. Your grocer may also carry one or two. If neither of these options work for you, try the Internet. Many reputable online merchants can deliver these mixes right to your door.

# Allergy-Friendly Icing

*When you know what's in your icing, it's easier to avoid allergens like milk and eggs. Use a splash of coffee for a warm brown color, beets for pinks and reds, blueberries for blue, strawberries for flavorful pinks, and lemon for the lightest of yellow tints.*

**INGREDIENTS | SERVES 8**

1 pound confectioners' sugar

2 tablespoons water

1 cup solid vegetable shortening

1 tablespoon vanilla extract

1 teaspoon butter flavoring

1 tablespoon meringue powder (optional)

1. Sift confectioners' sugar into a large mixing bowl. Cream remaining ingredients in a separate bowl.

2. Combine mixtures using an electric mixer set to medium speed for 2 minutes or until creamy and all ingredients are fully incorporated.

# Sugar-Free Frosting

*This recipe works for diabetics or others who are looking to limit their sugar intake. But don't let the low sugar content fool you—it's as sweet and delicious as you want it to be.*

**INGREDIENTS | 4 CUPS**

1 1.4-ounce package sugar-free instant vanilla pudding

1¾ cups milk

1 8-ounce package cream cheese

1 8-ounce tub frozen light whipped topping, thawed

1. In a steel mixing bowl, mix pudding mix and milk until lumps are gone. Set aside until mixture thickens.

2. Use an electric mixer to beat cream cheese until spreadable. Add pudding mixture to cream cheese and combine using electric mixer.

3. Fold in whipped topping and keep cool (not frozen) until ready to use.

# Gluten-Free Peach Cobbler

*This is a gluten-free recipe the whole family will want to share. Peaches and spice bake up with a buttery cake crust that just begs for a dollop of whipped topping or vanilla ice cream.*

**INGREDIENTS | SERVES 8**

1 quart canned peaches with liquid

2 cups gluten-free cake mix

½ cup soy milk

1 teaspoon cinnamon

½ teaspoon nutmeg

½ cup Fleischmann's margarine

1. Preheat oven to 350°F.

2. Pour canned peaches and liquid into a casserole dish.

3. Combine cake mix, soy milk, and spices in a small mixing bowl. Spoon this mixture on top of peaches in dish.

4. Cut margarine into pats and dot the top of the casserole. Bake for 15–20 minutes or until top looks golden brown.

# Diabetic-Friendly Hearth-Spice Angel Food Cake

*Angel food cake is a staple of many healthier diets. The delicate blend of spices in this recipe adds a little kick for variety.*

**INGREDIENTS | SERVES 6**

1 teaspoon cinnamon

1 teaspoon ground ginger

½ teaspoon ground nutmeg

1 18.25-ounce box angel food cake mix plus ingredients called for on box

Mix spices into dry cake mix. Prepare cake according to instructions on the package. Let cake cool in the pan before inverting onto a wire rack.

# Diabetic Carrot Cake

*While cakes can be made lower in sugars, they are not usually lower in carbohydrates. Enjoy them in moderation, taking special care to avoid cake recipes that contain fruit juice, which quickly raises blood sugar.*

**INGREDIENTS | SERVES 6**

1 18.25-ounce box spice cake mix

1 12-ounce can diet lemon-lime soft drink

½ cup shredded carrots

½ cup raisins

½ cup nuts, chopped

1. Preheat oven to 350°F. Grease and flour cake pan. Set aside.

2. Combine cake mix and diet soda, using electric mixer to blend completely. Fold in carrots, raisins, and nuts. Bake according to cake mix instructions. Allow cake to cool.

# Diabetic Lemon Cake

*Substituting diet soda for eggs and oil saves calories but lets the sweet flavor and tender texture shine right through. Add a splash of lemon juice to some sugar-free whipped topping to frost your fully cooled cake.*

**INGREDIENTS | SERVES 6**

1 18.25-ounce box lemon cake mix

1 12-ounce can lemon-lime diet carbonated soft drink

1. Preheat oven to 350°F. Grease and flour cake pan. Set aside.

2. Combine cake and soft drink to create a smooth batter. Turn batter into the cake pan. Bake according to cake mix instructions.

# Egg- and Dairy-Free Yellow Cake

*Three convenient ingredients stocked in your pantry means you're ready to bake anytime company stops by—or whenever the mood strikes.*

**INGREDIENTS | SERVES 6**

1 18.25-ounce box Duncan Hines Moist Deluxe Yellow Cake mix plus ingredients called for on box except eggs

6 teaspoons Ener-G Egg Replacer

8 tablespoons warm water

1 tub Duncan Hines French Vanilla Creamy Home-Style Frosting

Preheat oven to 350°F. Bake cake according to package instructions, substituting egg replacer and water for egg. Allow cake to cool completely before frosting with an egg- and dairy-free frosting.

# Orangey Angel Cookies

*These bright and yummy cookies are a tempting treat that can fit safely into a diabetic diet. Citrus adds a bright sweetness and the soda gives the dessert a celebratory color. Try this with sodas that don't contain any artificial colors.*

**INGREDIENTS | SERVES 28**

1 14½-ounce box angel food cake mix

½ cup diet orange soda

¼ teaspoon almond extract

1. Preheat oven to 350°F. Lightly treat cookie sheets with cooking spray.

2. Combine cake mix, orange soda, and almond extract in a large mixing bowl using an electric mixer set to medium speed. Mix to form a smooth, fully incorporated dough.

3. Spoon dough onto cookie sheets. Bake for 8 minutes. Remove from baking sheet to a wire rack for cooling. Serve and enjoy.

# Diabetic-Friendly Sweet Treat

*Finding a sweet indulgence that fits into a diabetic diet can be tricky. This one makes the choice easy and helps keep cravings under control. One serving equals 1 starch, 1 fruit, and 2 fats.*

**INGREDIENTS | SERVES 12**

1 18.25-ounce box white cake mix

1¾ cups sugar-free orange soda, divided use

¼ cup vegetable oil

2 eggs

1 1.3-ounce envelope dry whipped topping mix

1. Preheat oven to 350°F. Grease and flour a 13" × 9" cake pan.

2. In a large mixing bowl, beat cake mix, 1¼ cup orange soda, oil, and eggs for 3 minutes to form a smooth batter. Turn batter into cake pan and bake for 35 minutes.

3. Allow cake to cool before inverting onto a wire rack to cool completely.

4. Meanwhile, beat whipped topping mix and remaining ½ cup soda until stiff peaks form. Frost cake and store chilled until ready to serve.

# APPENDIX A

# Cake Decorating

# Basic Tools and Techniques

Most of the recipes in this book call for you to simply frost the cake. But if you really want to show off your creation, knowing how to decorate your cake will come in handy. First, there are a few necessary tools you'll want to keep around your kitchen.

To create designs or write words on your cake, you can buy decorating bags made of vinyl or even disposable plastic bags for more convenience. Spoon your frosting into the bag, filling it about halfway. Twist the top of the bag to seal and then squeeze firmly to move the frosting out through the decorating tip and onto your cake. It will take a bit of practice to become comfortable with the technique. A great way to practice using the different tips is to make designs on a sheet of waxed paper.

Some of the tools that you may want to collect are:

- Couplers—allow you to change decorating tips quickly and easily
- Fine writing tips—great for outlining parts of the cake, making scrolls and small dots, and writing
- Star tips—make nice mounds to put dragees on and create shells and other decorative effects
- Larger writing tips—great for polka dots and filling in larger areas with color
- Paintbrushes—can be used for applying egg yolk paint or corn syrup
- Toothpicks—can be used to move color or create a chevron effect when you drag them through stripes of thin frosting
- Special tools that allow you to make intricate sculptures with marzipan and fondant are fun to learn to use and will help you make spectacular decorated desserts.

Once the cake is decorated, set it aside to allow the frosting to harden before storing; this will keep the designs from smearing. A final garnish may be created by using products like luster dust or edible glitter to enhance the decorated cookie. Some people even use edible gold leaf for very special decorated cookies.

Edible gold and silver have been used for years all over the world. It is available in the United States, but the Food and Drug Administration (FDA) says that it has not been approved for human consumption. Edible gold and silver has been in use since before there was an FDA, so it was never submitted for premarket approval.

# Dusting and Stenciling Techniques

One of the easiest ways to decorate is to sift a fine coating of cocoa powder or confectioners' sugar onto your dessert. This technique is sometimes called dusting. To take this technique one step further, you can create a design on the top of your dessert by sifting cocoa powder or confectioners' sugar through a stencil.

1. You can use a paper doily as a stencil, or you can create a custom stencil by cutting a design out of sift paper or light cardboard.
2. If the top of your dessert is dry, you can lay the stencil directly on top. Place the cocoa powder or confectioners' sugar in a fine mesh sieve and gently tap, rather than shake, a thin even layer over the stencil. Take care to use a minimal amount. You want an even coverage, but if you use too much, the design will blur when you remove the stencil. Then slowly lift the stencil up, being careful not to disturb the design.
3. If the top of your dessert is moist or sticky, rig a frame that will hold the stencil above your dessert. You can do this by placing the dessert in a pan that is slightly larger and taller, or by arranging glasses or boxes around the dessert, upon which the stencil can rest.

If you've never used a stencil, it's a good idea to practice first by stenciling onto waxed paper. Once you've stenciled a few desserts, you'll have a feel for how much cocoa powder or confectioners' sugar to use and what stenciled designs look best.

Two more tips: Use alkalized ("Dutch-processed") cocoa powder for dusting and stenciling; it has a softer flavor. And don't be shy about blending cocoa powder and confectioners' sugar together. Adding ground nuts or spices provides varied effects and flavors.

# Chocolate Drizzles

This decorating technique works best on a cake that has already been covered with a smooth glaze. It creates an artistic random effect, like raindrops hitting your window on a windy day.

1. To prevent some of the mess this technique can create, set up a splatter shield by covering your immediate working area, including the walls, with waxed paper.
2. Melt couverture (chocolate rich in cocoa butter), stirring until smooth. While the chocolate is warm and very fluid, dip a fork in it, and quickly flick the fork over your dessert. Continue flicking in different directions until most of the chocolate has left the fork.
3. Dip the fork in the chocolate again and repeat until you achieve the effect you desire. With some desserts, you may want a light coverage, while with other desserts you may want more.
4. Allow the dessert to set in a cool room, or place in the refrigerator for 3 to 5 minutes.
5. When you're finished, place the waxed paper onto which the excess chocolate has fallen in the refrigerator until set.
6. Peel the bits of chocolate off the waxed paper and store to melt and use again, or save to break up and sprinkle on other desserts instead of the chocolate flavored sprinkles grocery stores sell.

# Piping

Perhaps one of the most widely used decorating techniques is piping. This can be used to create a wide variety of designs, including initials.

This technique requires a pastry bag fitted with a writing tip or a squeeze bottle with a very small opening. You can do this with frosting, royal icing, and special piping gels. If you want chocolate piping, use high-quality couverture for the best results. Melt the chocolate and place it in the pastry bag while it's still warm.

1. The easiest, and most popular, designs for piping are straight or diagonal lines, crosshatches, and swirls.
2. If you want very fine lines, choose a tip with a very small opening, make sure your piping material is very warm and fluid, and work quickly.
3. If you prefer heavier lines, let the material cool a bit and work more slowly, or select a tip with a slightly larger opening.
4. If the base glaze or coating on your dessert has not yet set, the material you pipe on top will melt into the base. If you want the decoration to sit on top of the base, wait until the base has set to decorate.

As with stenciling, if you've never piped before, practice on waxed paper.

## Filigree

This is a lovely decoration that's surprisingly simple to do if you have a template. Filigree is a design piped in a delicate, usually loopy, design, and placed vertically or horizontally on a dessert. It can be made using royal icing or melted chocolate. You can even create multidimensional decorations by piping flat pieces and gluing them together with melted chocolate.

1. The easiest way to create filigree is to place a picture of the design you'd like to duplicate on a flat surface under a sheet of waxed paper or cooking-grade acetate.
2. Place the filigree material in a pastry bag fitted with a writing tip and trace the design. Allow the filigree to set in a cool room, or refrigerate for 3 to 5 minutes.
3. Carefully remove the filigree from the waxed paper or acetate with a metal spatula. Try not to touch the piece too much; this prevents fingerprints and melting.
4. Place on a cake or store in an airtight container in a cool place. If you need to stack the pieces, place a piece of waxed paper between each layer.

## Appliqués

Similar to filigree or stained glass, with this decoration you pipe an outline of an object (for example, a butterfly) and then color in the center.

1. Place a picture of the object you want to copy on a cookie sheet or jellyroll pan under a sheet of waxed paper or acetate.
2. Place melted chocolate or icing in a pastry bag fitted with a writing tip. Outline the object.
3. Allow the outline to set in a cool room, or refrigerate for 3 to 5 minutes.
4. Place melted chocolate or icing of another color in a pastry bag fitted with a writing tip. Lightly fill in the area within the outlines with chocolate.
5. Quickly lift and tap the cookie sheet after you fill each small object or each area of a larger object; the newly piped material should spread and flatten, filling in any small gaps.
6. Refrigerate for 3 to 5 minutes, or until set.
7. Carefully remove the appliqués from the waxed paper or acetate with a metal spatula.
8. Handle and store these decorations as you would filigree.

## Grated Chocolate

Grated chocolate can be folded into a batter, much like chocolate chips, or used to decorate desserts or drinks.

1. Chill a bar or block of couverture. Line a jellyroll pan with waxed paper.
2. Draw the chocolate over the holes of a stainless-steel hand-held grater onto the waxed paper.
3. Store the grated chocolate in an airtight container in a cool place.

# Shaved Chocolate

Shaving chocolate with a vegetable peeler or a knife is one way of creating chocolate curls.

1. To create the smallest chocolate curls: Chill a bar or block of couverture. Line a jellyroll pan with waxed paper.
2. Prop the chocolate on the edge of the jellyroll pan so that the curls will fall onto the waxed paper. Draw a vegetable peeler over the chocolate lightly and quickly.
3. For slightly larger curls: Allow the chocolate to warm slightly at room temperature. Draw the vegetable peeler over the chocolate a little more slowly, applying a little more pressure.
4. For wider chocolate curls: Prop a block of chocolate on the edge of a jellyroll pan lined with waxed paper.
5. Place a large chef's knife at the base of the chocolate block. Hold the handle of the knife with one hand and the tip of the blade with the other, so the blade of the knife is parallel to the surface of the chocolate. (If you've never used this technique, place a cardboard sleeve over the tip of the knife so you don't cut yourself.)
6. Draw the knife up from the base of the chocolate block. Once again, the temperature of the chocolate and the amount of pressure you apply will determine the size and weight of the shaved curls.
7. Store shaved chocolate in an airtight container, in a cool place.

# Chocolate Curls

The other method for creating chocolate curls is to spread and scrape melted chocolate. With this technique, you can use one type of chocolate, creating solid color curls, or you can blend chocolate of different colors, creating marbled, feathered, or striped curls. For a scraping tool you can use a spatula, chef's knife, plastic putty knife, or almost anything with a clean, dry straight edge.

1. For this technique you will need stainless-steel cookie sheets or jellyroll pans with perfectly flat, clean backs. Warm the pans on a low heat in your oven. This prevents the melted chocolate from cooling too quickly while spreading a thin layer. Be careful not to let the pans get too hot; you should be able to handle them without oven mitts.
2. To create solid color curls: Spread the melted chocolate in a thin (approximately ⅛-inch-thick), even layer on the back of the warmed pans. Tap the pans gently to release air bubbles and to smooth the finish.
3. Refrigerate for about 15 to 20 minutes, or until set. Remove from the refrigerator and warm at room temperature until you can scrape the chocolate without it cracking or splintering. If it gets too warm, refrigerate it for a few more minutes.
4. The size and shape of the curls depends on the scraping tool you use, the temperature of the chocolate, and the angle at which you scrape. The wider the blade or straight edge, the wider the chocolate curls. The softer the chocolate, the tighter the curl. The sharper the angle of your blade, the tighter the curl. For example, to create chocolate cigarettes, scrape at a 45-degree angle.
5. Secure the pan so it will not slide or shift as you scrape. Place your scraping tool at the top of the pan and gently slide your scraping tool over the chocolate. Place the curls on your dessert or in an airtight container layered with sheets of waxed paper.

## Striped Chocolate Curls

1. To create curls with thin stripes: Warm the pans.
2. Spread a thin layer of chocolate on the back of a pan. Chill until set.
3. Scrape a series a fine lines into the chocolate using a pastry comb. If you're having trouble keeping the lines straight, place a metal ruler or straight edge alongside the chocolate to guide your pastry comb.
4. Lift and gently tap the excess chocolate onto waxed paper to recycle.
5. Spread a contrasting color of melted chocolate over the remaining chocolate lines. Refrigerate until set and scrape.
6. For wider stripes: Melt contrasting colors of chocolate separately. Using pastry bags fitted with plain ¼-inch tips, pipe parallel stripes of

chocolate about ¼ inch apart on the back of warmed pans. Using a spatula, carefully spread the lines so they blend together. Proceed as you would for solid color curls.

7. For random stripes: Melt contrasting colors of chocolate separately. Spread a thin layer of chocolate on the back of a warmed pan. Randomly drizzle a contrasting color of chocolate on top. Proceed as you would for solid color curls.

## Feathered Chocolate Curls

1. To create a feathered effect: Warm the pans.
2. Spread a thin layer of chocolate on the back of a pan.
3. Working quickly with a contrasting color of chocolate, pipe evenly-spaced parallel lines of chocolate, using a pastry bag fitted with a writing tip.
4. Using a toothpick or small sable paintbrush, gently run a line perpendicularly from left to right through one of the piped lines. Change direction, running a line from right to left, through the next piped line. Repeat, alternating directions, until all the lines are feathered.
5. Tap, chill, and scrape, as you would for solid color curls.
6. To create feathered hearts: Pipe or spoon small circles of chocolate in a parallel line. Run a toothpick or brush through the center of the circles to create a line of hearts. Tap, chill, and scrape, as you would for solid color curls.

## Marbled Chocolate Curls

1. To create a marbled effect: Warm the pans.
2. Spread a thin layer of chocolate on the back of a pan.
3. Working quickly with a contrasting color of chocolate, lightly pipe random lines or swirls of chocolate using a pastry bag fitted with a writing tip. (Or drizzle the contrasting color on top.)
4. Using a toothpick or small sable paintbrush, gently swirl the chocolates together.
5. Tap, chill, and scrape, as you would for solid color curls.

# Chocolate Fans

Chocolate fans can be made with pure chocolate for a crisp look, or with chocolate dough for a softer look. In either case, they can be made in a variety of sizes and designs.

1. Warm a pan, melt and spread the chocolate, and chill as you would for solid, striped, feathered, or marbled chocolate curls.
2. After chilling, brace the pan to prevent it from shifting as you work. Hold the bottom of a spatula or straightedge blade in one hand and the top edge in the other, at a slight angle (about 10 degrees) to the pan.
3. Scrape sections of the chocolate in a slight arc, or fan shape, with one end of the scraper moving faster than the other. One side of the fan should have soft ruffles, while the other should come together in a tight gather. Gently pinch the gathered end before chilling again to set.

# Chocolate Leaves

Chocolate leaves are fairly simple and fun to make. They can also be made in a variety of shapes and sizes to reflect the season or theme of your dessert. They can be scattered, placed symmetrically, or even clustered in a large, open, rose bloom shape.

Be careful to use leaves of edible plants that are clean, dry, and free of pesticides.

1. Line several cookie sheets or jellyroll pans with waxed paper.
2. Paint the top (shiny side) of the leaves with melted chocolate, using a paintbrush, small pastry brush, or your finger. Be careful not to get any chocolate on the edges of the leaves, which will make it more difficult to peel the leaf off after the chocolate has set.
3. Place the leaves chocolate side up on the waxed paper. Refrigerate until set.
4. Gently peel the fresh leaves off the chocolate leaves, and place on your dessert, or store in an airtight container layered with waxed paper.

# Chocolate Cutouts

Chocolate cutouts can turn a simple dessert into something special. They can also help you incorporate a theme into your dessert.

1. Proceed as you would for solid, striped, feathered, or marbled chocolate curls.
2. Refrigerate for a few minutes, until firm but not yet set.
3. If you are using metal cookie cutters to create shapes, gently press the cookie cutters into the chocolate. If you need squares, rectangles, or triangles, score the chocolate with a knife. Chill until set.
4. Remove from refrigerator, fit the cookie cutters (or knife) into the preformed shapes, and gently cut through the chocolate. Place on your dessert, or store in an airtight container, layered with waxed paper.

# Substitutions and Conversions

# Common Baking Substitutions

**Allspice:** For each teaspoon, use ½ teaspoon cinnamon, ¼ teaspoon ginger, and ¼ teaspoon cloves.

**Baking powder:** For each teaspoon, use ½ teaspoon cream of tartar and ¼ teaspoon baking soda.

**Beer:** For each cup, use 1 cup chicken broth.

**Brandy:** For each ¼ cup, use 1 teaspoon imitation brandy extract plus enough water to make ¼ cup.

**Brown sugar:** For each cup, use 1 cup granulated sugar plus ¼ cup molasses (decrease amount of liquid in recipe by ¼ cup).

**Butter (salted):** For each cup, use 1 cup margarine.

**Butter (unsalted):** For each cup, use 1 cup shortening.

**Buttermilk:** For each cup, place 1 tablespoon lemon juice or vinegar in the bottom of a measuring cup and fill with milk. Let stand 5 minutes.

**Cardamom:** Use an equal amount of ginger.

**Cheddar cheese:** For each cup, use 1 cup Colby Cheddar or Monterey Jack cheese.

**Chocolate (semisweet):** For each ounce, use 1 ounce unsweetened chocolate plus 4 teaspoons sugar.

**Chocolate (unsweetened):** For each ounce, use 3 tablespoons unsweetened cocoa and 1 tablespoon melted butter.

**Cinnamon:** Use ½ the amount of nutmeg.

**Cloves:** Use double the amount of cinnamon and a little cayenne pepper.

**Cocoa:** For each ¼ cup, use 1 ounce unsweetened chocolate.

**Corn syrup:** For each cup, use 1 cup granulated sugar and ¼ cup water; bring to a boil and boil 1 minute. Set aside.

**Cream (half and half):** For each cup, use 1 tablespoon vegetable oil or melted butter and enough whole milk to make a cup.

**Cream (heavy):** For each cup, use ¾ cup milk and ⅓ cup butter.

**Cream (light):** For each cup, use ¾ cup milk and 3 tablespoons butter.

**Cream (whipped):** For each cup, use 1 cup frozen whipped topping, thawed.

**Cream cheese:** For each cup, use 1 cup pureéd cottage cheese.

**Cream of tartar:** For each teaspoon, use 2 teaspoons lemon juice.

**Egg:** For each egg, use 2 egg whites or 2 egg yolks or ¼ cup egg substitute.

**Evaporated milk:** For each cup, use 1 cup light cream.

**Gelatin:** For each tablespoon, use 2 teaspoons agar.

**Ginger:** Use an equal amount of cinnamon and a pinch of cayenne pepper.

**Granulated sugar:** For each cup, use 1 cup brown sugar.

**Honey:** For each cup, use 1¼ cups granulated sugar and ¼ cup water.

**Lemon juice:** For each teaspoon, use ½ teaspoon vinegar.

**Lemon zest:** For each teaspoon, use ½ teaspoon lemon extract.

**Lime juice:** For each teaspoon, use 1 teaspoon vinegar.

**Lime zest:** For each teaspoon, use 1 teaspoon lemon zest.

**Margarine:** For each cup, use 1 cup shortening and ½ teaspoon salt.

**Mayonnaise:** For each cup, use 1 cup sour cream or plain yogurt.

**Milk (whole):** For each cup, use 1 cup soy milk or rice milk.

**Molasses:** For each cup, use ½ cup honey, ½ cup brown sugar, and ¼ cup water.

**Nutmeg:** Use ½ the amount of cinnamon and ¼ amount of ginger.

**Orange juice:** For each tablespoon, use 1 tablespoon lemon or lime juice.

**Orange zest:** For each tablespoon, use 1 teaspoon lemon juice.

**Parmesan cheese:** For each ½ cup, use ½ cup Asiago or Romano cheese.

**Pepperoni:** For each ounce, use 1 ounce salami.

**Pumpkin pie spice:** For each teaspoon, mix ½ teaspoon cinnamon, ¼ teaspoon ginger, ⅛ teaspoon cloves, and ⅛ teaspoon grated nutmeg.

**Raisins:** For each cup, use 1 cup dried cranberries.

**Ricotta cheese:** For each cup, use 1 cup dry cottage cheese.

**Rum:** For each tablespoon, use ½ teaspoon rum extract plus enough water to make 1 tablespoon.

**Semisweet chocolate chips:** For each cup, use 1 cup chocolate candies.

**Shortening:** For each cup, use 1 cup butter.

**Sour cream:** For each cup, use 1 cup plain yogurt.

**Sweetened condensed milk:** For each 14-ounce can, use ¾ cup granulated sugar, ½ cup water, and ⅛ cup dry powdered milk; boil and cook, stirring frequently, until thickened, about 20 minutes.

**Vegetable oil:** For each cup, use 1 cup applesauce.

**Vinegar:** For each teaspoon, use 1 teaspoon lemon or lime juice.

**Wine:** For each cup, use 1 cup chicken broth.

**Yogurt:** For each cup, use 1 cup sour cream.

# U.S. Volume Equivalents

| | | | | | | | | |
|---|---|---|---|---|---|---|---|---|
| 1½ teaspoons | = | ½ tablespoon | | | | | | |
| 3 teaspoons | = | 1 tablespoon | | | | | | |
| 2 tablespoons | = | 1 ounce | = | ⅛ cup | | | | |
| 8 ounces | = | 16 tablespoons | = | 1 cup | | | | |
| 2 cups | = | 1 pint | = | 16 ounces | | | | |
| 2 pints | = | 1 quart | = | 4 cups | = | 32 ounces |
| 4 quarts | = | 1 gallon | = | 16 cups | = | 128 ounces |

# U.S. Volume to Metric Volume

| | | |
|---|---|---|
| ¼ teaspoon | = | 1.23 ml |
| ½ teaspoon | = | 2.5 ml |
| ¾ teaspoon | = | 3.7 ml |
| 1 teaspoon | = | 4.9 ml |
| 1½ teaspoons | = | 7.5 ml |
| 2 teaspoons | = | 10 ml |
| 3 teaspoons | = | 15 ml |
| ⅛ cup | = | 30 ml |
| ¼ cup | = | 60 ml |
| ½ cup | = | 120 ml |
| ¾ cup | = | 180 ml |
| 1 cup | = | 240 ml |
| 2 cups | = | 480 ml |
| 2¼ cups | = | 540 ml |

| | | |
|---|---|---|
| 2½ cups | = | 600 ml |
| 2¾ cups | = | 660 ml |
| 3 cups | = | 720 ml |
| 4 cups | = | 960 ml |
| 4 quarts | = | 3.8 l |

## U.S. Weight Measurements to Metric Weight Measurements

| | | |
|---|---|---|
| ½ ounce | = | 14 grams |
| 1 ounce | = | 29 grams |
| 1½ ounces | = | 43 grams |
| 2 ounces | = | 57 grams |
| 4 ounces | = | 113 grams |
| 8 ounces | = | 227 grams |
| 16 ounces | = | 454 grams |
| 32 ounces | = | 907 grams |
| 64 ounces | = | 1.8 kilograms |

# Vegan Substitutions

Cooking vegan doesn't always mean abandoning all your favorite old recipes. In some cases you'll be able to replace milk with soy milk, butter with margarine, and eggs with Ener-g Egg replacer, or banana. (Use one banana per egg called for in recipe.)

It's also possible to find vegan cake mixes.

P.E.T.A., the organization famous for protecting animals and animal rights, keeps a list of vegan convenience foods on its website under the name "Accidentally Vegan." On this list you will find a few cake mixes, pudding mixes, and prepared frosting that are readily available in most groceries and completely vegan. Unexpected listings include:

- Duncan Hines California Walnut Brownie Mix

- Duncan Hines Creamy Home-Style Frosting (Chocolate)

- Duncan Hines Creamy Home-Style Frosting (Classic Vanilla)

- Duncan Hines Creamy Home-Style Frosting (French Vanilla)

- Ghirardelli Chocolate Chip Cookie Mix

- Jell-O Instant Pudding (Pistachio)

- Jell-O Instant Pudding (Banana Creme)

- Jell-O Instant Pudding (Chocolate)

- Jell-O Instant Pudding (Lemon)

- Jell-O Instant Pudding (Vanilla)

# APPENDIX C

# Glossary

### Baking pan

A flat pan, usually metal, that may or may not have a lip around the edge.

### Beat

To make a mixture smooth by briskly stirring with a whisk, spoon, or electric beater.

### Blend

To gently mix ingredients until they are completely mixed.

### Boil

To bring a liquid to the temperature that causes bubbles to rise to the surface and break in a steady stream.

### Cream

To beat butter or shortening until it has a light, fluffy consistency. Air is incorporated into the fat so the texture is lighter and fluffier.

### Drizzle

To quickly pour a glaze over a baked item randomly and in a thin stream.

### Dust

To lightly coat a baked good with powdered sugar.

### Extract

Flavoring products that are made from the essential oil of a plant. These concentrated oils are generally suspended in alcohol.

Examples are: vanilla, anise, almond, lemon, mint. Extracts are higher quality than flavorings and are preferred in these recipes.

## Flavoring

Imitation extracts which are created in laboratories from chemicals. A flavoring does not have to contain any part of the item it mimics and is often completely artificial.

## Fold

To gently mix ingredients. Generally, the dry ingredients are sifted over the top of the whipped or beaten ingredients and then a rubber spatula is used to cut through the mixture. The spatula is then moved across the bottom and brought up the other side, folding the mixture back on itself.

## Food Coloring

Food-grade dyes which are used to tint various foods. Paste food colors are the best, and give the most intense color.

## Glaze

A thin type of frosting that is used to add extra flavor to a cookie or cake.

## Gluten

A protein present in all flour, but especially in wheat flour. It provides an elastic structure for baked goods. Many people are allergic to it and must not eat it.

## Gluten-free baking mix

A baking mix that is free of gluten and nonallergenic.

## Pipe

To force frosting or filling through a pastry bag.

## Shortening

A solid fat made from vegetable oils. Shortening has been criticized for the high amounts of trans fatty acids it has had in the past. Manufacturers are now making it without the trans fats, or with reduced trans fats. You can also get organic shortenings that have no trans fats.

## Sift

To shake flour or powdered sugar through a sifter to make it light and fluffy and to remove lumps.

## Vanilla bean

Vanilla beans are the seed pods of a special orchid plant from which vanilla is made. It can be placed in a canister with sugar to flavor the sugar.

## Whip

To beat a food, usually cream or egg whites, rapidly enough to incorporate air and cause the food to double or triple in volume.

## Zest

The outer, colored portion of a citrus fruit. It is grated and added to foods to flavor them.

# Resources

## All Recipes

This site has an uncountable number of recipes, and each recipe has an area for comments so you can find out if it worked for other people or not. Excellent search features and other user-friendly items make this online cookbook invaluable.
*http://allrecipes.com*

## Bakers' Nook

Thousands of pans, decorations, and cookie cutters to help you create incredible baked goods.
*www.shopbakersnook.com*

## Bakespace

Bakespace is a social networking site for foodies. Socialize, have your questions answered, and find new recipes as well as new friends.
*http://bakespace.com*

## Baking Delights

This site is where I post my own recipes on at least a daily basis and answer readers' questions.
*www.bakingdelights.com*

## Converting Recipes

This is an excellent resource for those who do not use the same measurements as those used in the United States. You can easily convert any recipe with these charts.
*www.jsward.com/cooking/conversion.shtml*

## Cook's Thesaurus

Thousands of suggestions for food substitutions in one place. A great resource.
*www.foodsubs.com*

### Daring Bakers Blog Roll

This site lists over 1,000 blogs of the members of Daring Bakers. Daring Bakers is a group of bloggers that create the same challenging recipe every month. The recipes that you will find on the various sites are top notch.
*http://thedaringkitchen.com/member-blogs*

### Group Recipes

Another networking site for people who love to cook. Plenty of recipes to choose from.
*www.grouprecipes.com*

### Kitchen Kraft

Kitchen Kraft is a huge site with every item imaginable to make your baking more creative, easier, and more fun.
*www.kitchenkrafts.com*

### Nutritional Information Calculator

Enter the ingredients of any recipe and find out the calories, carbs, proteins, and other nutritional information.
*http://recipes.sparkpeople.com/recipe-calculator.asp*

### Penzeys Spices

Wonderful, fresh spices and herbs for your cooking and baking needs.
*http://penzeys.com/cgi-bin/penzeys/shophome.html*

### Wilton

Baking supplies of all types. A huge variety of paste food colorings, icing bags, decorator tips, and inspiration.
*www.wilton.com*

# Index

Mozzarella cheese, 72
Mushrooms, sliced, can, 77

## N

Nutmeg, 50, 66, 73, 187, 203, 211, 243, 244
Nuts, 59, 84, 93, 103, 171, 245

## O

Oatmeal, 125, 134
  quick cooking, 73
Oats
  quick-cooking, 126
  rolled, 135
Oil
  olive, 121, 171, 173, 242
  safflower, 198
  vegetable, 12, 19, 25, 28, 36, 45, 46, 51, 55, 58, 66, 69, 75, 77, 82, 83, 87, 88, 90, 92, 94, 101, 103, 104, 107, 114, 125, 134, 136, 138, 139, 141, 142, 153, 154, 156, 159, 160, 161, 168, 175, 176, 183, 186, 187, 190, 191, 195, 196, 197, 204, 209, 213, 215, 216, 225, 247
Onion, 76, 77, 78
  green, 77
  powder, 70
Orange, 82
  extract, 92, 173
  flavored cake mix, 216
  juice, 38, 215, 242

soda, 246
soda, sugar-free, 247
Oranges, 122, 215
  mandarin, canned, 96, 98, 109
Oregano, 76

## P

Parmesan cheese, 76
Peach
  baby food, 22
  pie filling, 50, 73, 105, 122
  schnapps, 107
Peaches, 218
  can, sliced in syrup, 49, 107, 244
Peanut brittle, 64
Peanut butter, 57, 139, 147, 185
  creamy, 30
  crunchy, 127, 128, 139, 153
  cups, 37
  morsels, 135
Peanuts, 104
Pecans, 17, 51, 63, 73, 79, 107, 136, 140, 153, 186, 190, 202, 203, 211
Pectin, 217
Pepper, 69, 70
  cayenne, 70
Peppermint flavor, organic, 219
Pepperoni, 72
Pie filling, unspecified type, 123
Pineapple

candied, 190
crushed, 17, 36, 54, 97, 98, 102, 109, 154, 230
juice, 40, 190
Pizza crust, refrigerated, 70
Plum baby food, 28
Plums, canned, pitted with liquid, 101
Poppyseeds, 87
Potato starch, 238
Pound cake mix, organic, 221
Pralines, 153
Preheating, 9
Preserves, freezer, 219
Pudding mix, 12, 166
  banana, 90, 102
  butterscotch, 216
  chocolate, 41, 46, 101, 112, 114, 158, 170, 172, 175, 176, 181
  French vanilla, 44, 154
  lemon, 14, 52, 61
  organic, 218
  pistachio, 196
  vanilla, 14, 19, 33, 51, 53, 66, 82, 103, 107, 109, 178, 190, 195, 204, 232, 233, 242
  vanilla, sugar-free, 243
  yellow, 215
Pumpkin, 212
  canned, 56, 163, 202
  pie spice, 56, 158, 214
  purée, 225
  purée, organic, 229, 232

166, 173, 176, 177, 178, 182,
185, 192, 194, 200, 203, 228,
229, 230, 236, 237, 238, 239,
240, 242, 243

# THE EVERYTHING SERIES!

## BUSINESS & PERSONAL FINANCE

Everything® Accounting Book
Everything® Budgeting Book, 2nd Ed.
Everything® Business Planning Book
Everything® Coaching and Mentoring Book, 2nd Ed.
Everything® Fundraising Book
Everything® Get Out of Debt Book
Everything® Grant Writing Book, 2nd Ed.
Everything® Guide to Buying Foreclosures
**Everything® Guide to Fundraising, $15.95**
Everything® Guide to Mortgages
Everything® Guide to Personal Finance for Single Mothers
Everything® Home-Based Business Book, 2nd Ed.
**Everything® Homebuying Book, 3rd Ed., $15.95**
Everything® Homeselling Book, 2nd Ed.
Everything® Human Resource Management Book
Everything® Improve Your Credit Book
Everything® Investing Book, 2nd Ed.
Everything® Landlording Book
Everything® Leadership Book, 2nd Ed.
Everything® Managing People Book, 2nd Ed.
Everything® Negotiating Book
Everything® Online Auctions Book
Everything® Online Business Book
Everything® Personal Finance Book
Everything® Personal Finance in Your 20s & 30s Book, 2nd Ed.
**Everything® Personal Finance in Your 40s & 50s Book, $15.95**
Everything® Project Management Book, 2nd Ed.
Everything® Real Estate Investing Book
Everything® Retirement Planning Book
Everything® Robert's Rules Book, $7.95
Everything® Selling Book
Everything® Start Your Own Business Book, 2nd Ed.
Everything® Wills & Estate Planning Book

## COOKING

Everything® Barbecue Cookbook
Everything® Bartender's Book, 2nd Ed., $9.95
Everything® Calorie Counting Cookbook
Everything® Cheese Book
Everything® Chinese Cookbook
Everything® Classic Recipes Book
Everything® Cocktail Parties & Drinks Book
Everything® College Cookbook
Everything® Cooking for Baby and Toddler Book
Everything® Diabetes Cookbook
Everything® Easy Gourmet Cookbook
Everything® Fondue Cookbook
**Everything® Food Allergy Cookbook, $15.95**
Everything® Fondue Party Book
Everything® Gluten-Free Cookbook
Everything® Glycemic Index Cookbook
Everything® Grilling Cookbook
**Everything® Healthy Cooking for Parties Book, $15.95**
Everything® Holiday Cookbook
Everything® Indian Cookbook
Everything® Lactose-Free Cookbook
Everything® Low-Cholesterol Cookbook

**Everything® Low-Fat High-Flavor Cookbook, 2nd Ed., $15.95**
Everything® Low-Salt Cookbook
Everything® Meals for a Month Cookbook
Everything® Meals on a Budget Cookbook
Everything® Mediterranean Cookbook
Everything® Mexican Cookbook
Everything® No Trans Fat Cookbook
**Everything® One-Pot Cookbook, 2nd Ed., $15.95**
**Everything® Organic Cooking for Baby & Toddler Book, $15.95**
Everything® Pizza Cookbook
**Everything® Quick Meals Cookbook, 2nd Ed., $15.95**
Everything® Slow Cooker Cookbook
Everything® Slow Cooking for a Crowd Cookbook
Everything® Soup Cookbook
Everything® Stir-Fry Cookbook
Everything® Sugar-Free Cookbook
Everything® Tapas and Small Plates Cookbook
Everything® Tex-Mex Cookbook
Everything® Thai Cookbook
Everything® Vegetarian Cookbook
Everything® Whole-Grain, High-Fiber Cookbook
Everything® Wild Game Cookbook
Everything® Wine Book, 2nd Ed.

## GAMES

Everything® 15-Minute Sudoku Book, $9.95
Everything® 30-Minute Sudoku Book, $9.95
Everything® Bible Crosswords Book, $9.95
Everything® Blackjack Strategy Book
Everything® Brain Strain Book, $9.95
Everything® Bridge Book
Everything® Card Games Book
Everything® Card Tricks Book, $9.95
Everything® Casino Gambling Book, 2nd Ed.
Everything® Chess Basics Book
**Everything® Christmas Crosswords Book, $9.95**
Everything® Craps Strategy Book
Everything® Crossword and Puzzle Book
**Everything® Crosswords and Puzzles for Quote Lovers Book, $9.95**
Everything® Crossword Challenge Book
Everything® Crosswords for the Beach Book, $9.95
Everything® Cryptic Crosswords Book, $9.95
Everything® Cryptograms Book, $9.95
Everything® Easy Crosswords Book
Everything® Easy Kakuro Book, $9.95
Everything® Easy Large-Print Crosswords Book
Everything® Games Book, 2nd Ed.
**Everything® Giant Book of Crosswords**
Everything® Giant Sudoku Book, $9.95
Everything® Giant Word Search Book
Everything® Kakuro Challenge Book, $9.95
Everything® Large-Print Crossword Challenge Book
Everything® Large-Print Crosswords Book
**Everything® Large-Print Travel Crosswords Book**
Everything® Lateral Thinking Puzzles Book, $9.95
Everything® Literary Crosswords Book, $9.95
Everything® Mazes Book
Everything® Memory Booster Puzzles Book, $9.95

Everything® Movie Crosswords Book, $9.95
Everything® Music Crosswords Book, $9.95
Everything® Online Poker Book
Everything® Pencil Puzzles Book, $9.95
Everything® Poker Strategy Book
Everything® Pool & Billiards Book
Everything® Puzzles for Commuters Book, $9.95
Everything® Puzzles for Dog Lovers Book, $9.95
Everything® Sports Crosswords Book, $9.95
Everything® Test Your IQ Book, $9.95
Everything® Texas Hold 'Em Book, $9.95
Everything® Travel Crosswords Book, $9.95
**Everything® Travel Mazes Book, $9.95**
**Everything® Travel Word Search Book, $9.95**
Everything® TV Crosswords Book, $9.95
Everything® Word Games Challenge Book
Everything® Word Scramble Book
Everything® Word Search Book

## HEALTH

Everything® Alzheimer's Book
Everything® Diabetes Book
Everything® First Aid Book, $9.95
**Everything® Green Living Book**
**Everything® Health Guide to Addiction and Recovery**
Everything® Health Guide to Adult Bipolar Disorder
Everything® Health Guide to Arthritis
Everything® Health Guide to Controlling Anxiety
Everything® Health Guide to Depression
**Everything® Health Guide to Diabetes, 2nd Ed.**
Everything® Health Guide to Fibromyalgia
Everything® Health Guide to Menopause, 2nd Ed.
Everything® Health Guide to Migraines
**Everything® Health Guide to Multiple Sclerosis**
Everything® Health Guide to OCD
Everything® Health Guide to PMS
Everything® Health Guide to Postpartum Care
Everything® Health Guide to Thyroid Disease
Everything® Hypnosis Book
Everything® Low Cholesterol Book
Everything® Menopause Book
Everything® Nutrition Book
Everything® Reflexology Book
Everything® Stress Management Book
**Everything® Superfoods Book, $15.95**

## HISTORY

Everything® American Government Book
Everything® American History Book, 2nd Ed.
**Everything® American Revolution Book, $15.95**
Everything® Civil War Book
Everything® Freemasons Book
Everything® Irish History & Heritage Book
Everything® World War II Book, 2nd Ed.

## HOBBIES

Everything® Candlemaking Book
Everything® Cartooning Book
Everything® Coin Collecting Book
Everything® Digital Photography Book, 2nd Ed.

Everything® Drawing Book
Everything® Family Tree Book, 2nd Ed.
**Everything® Guide to Online Genealogy, $15.95**
Everything® Knitting Book
Everything® Knots Book
Everything® Photography Book
Everything® Quilting Book
Everything® Sewing Book
Everything® Soapmaking Book, 2nd Ed.
Everything® Woodworking Book

## HOME IMPROVEMENT

Everything® Feng Shui Book
Everything® Feng Shui Decluttering Book, $9.95
Everything® Fix-It Book
Everything® Green Living Book
Everything® Home Decorating Book
Everything® Home Storage Solutions Book
Everything® Homebuilding Book
Everything® Organize Your Home Book, 2nd Ed.

## KIDS' BOOKS

All titles are $7.95
Everything® Fairy Tales Book, $14.95
Everything® Kids' Animal Puzzle & Activity Book
Everything® Kids' Astronomy Book
Everything® Kids' Baseball Book, 5th Ed.
Everything® Kids' Bible Trivia Book
Everything® Kids' Bugs Book
Everything® Kids' Cars and Trucks Puzzle and Activity Book
Everything® Kids' Christmas Puzzle & Activity Book
Everything® Kids' Connect the Dots
    Puzzle and Activity Book
**Everything® Kids' Cookbook, 2nd Ed.**
Everything® Kids' Crazy Puzzles Book
Everything® Kids' Dinosaurs Book
**Everything® Kids' Dragons Puzzle and Activity Book**
Everything® Kids' Environment Book $7.95
Everything® Kids' Fairies Puzzle and Activity Book
Everything® Kids' First Spanish Puzzle and Activity Book
Everything® Kids' Football Book
**Everything® Kids' Geography Book**
Everything® Kids' Gross Cookbook
Everything® Kids' Gross Hidden Pictures Book
Everything® Kids' Gross Jokes Book
Everything® Kids' Gross Mazes Book
Everything® Kids' Gross Puzzle & Activity Book
Everything® Kids' Halloween Puzzle & Activity Book
**Everything® Kids' Hanukkah Puzzle and Activity Book**
Everything® Kids' Hidden Pictures Book
Everything® Kids' Horses Book
Everything® Kids' Joke Book
Everything® Kids' Knock Knock Book
Everything® Kids' Learning French Book
Everything® Kids' Learning Spanish Book
Everything® Kids' Magical Science Experiments Book
Everything® Kids' Math Puzzles Book
Everything® Kids' Mazes Book
**Everything® Kids' Money Book, 2nd Ed.**
**Everything® Kids' Mummies, Pharaoh's, and Pyramids
    Puzzle and Activity Book**
Everything® Kids' Nature Book
Everything® Kids' Pirates Puzzle and Activity Book
Everything® Kids' Presidents Book
Everything® Kids' Princess Puzzle and Activity Book
Everything® Kids' Puzzle Book

Everything® Kids' Racecars Puzzle and Activity Book
Everything® Kids' Riddles & Brain Teasers Book
Everything® Kids' Science Experiments Book
Everything® Kids' Sharks Book
Everything® Kids' Soccer Book
**Everything® Kids' Spelling Book**
Everything® Kids' Spies Puzzle and Activity Book
Everything® Kids' States Book
Everything® Kids' Travel Activity Book
Everything® Kids' Word Search Puzzle and Activity Book

## LANGUAGE

Everything® Conversational Japanese Book with CD, $19.95
Everything® French Grammar Book
Everything® French Phrase Book, $9.95
Everything® French Verb Book, $9.95
**Everything® German Phrase Book, $9.95**
Everything® German Practice Book with CD, $19.95
Everything® Inglés Book
Everything® Intermediate Spanish Book with CD, $19.95
**Everything® Italian Phrase Book, $9.95**
Everything® Italian Practice Book with CD, $19.95
Everything® Learning Brazilian Portuguese Book with CD, $19.95
Everything® Learning French Book with CD, 2nd Ed., $19.95
Everything® Learning German Book
Everything® Learning Italian Book
Everything® Learning Latin Book
Everything® Learning Russian Book with CD, $19.95
Everything® Learning Spanish Book
Everything® Learning Spanish Book with CD, 2nd Ed., $19.95
Everything® Russian Practice Book with CD, $19.95
**Everything® Sign Language Book, $15.95**
Everything® Spanish Grammar Book
Everything® Spanish Phrase Book, $9.95
Everything® Spanish Practice Book with CD, $19.95
Everything® Spanish Verb Book, $9.95
Everything® Speaking Mandarin Chinese Book with CD, $19.95

## MUSIC

Everything® Bass Guitar Book with CD, $19.95
Everything® Drums Book with CD, $19.95
Everything® Guitar Book with CD, 2nd Ed., $19.95
Everything® Guitar Chords Book with CD, $19.95
**Everything® Guitar Scales Book with CD, $19.95**
Everything® Harmonica Book with CD, $15.95
Everything® Home Recording Book
Everything® Music Theory Book with CD, $19.95
Everything® Reading Music Book with CD, $19.95
Everything® Rock & Blues Guitar Book with CD, $19.95
Everything® Rock & Blues Piano Book with CD, $19.95
**Everything® Rock Drums Book with CD, $19.95**
**Everything® Singing Book with CD, $19.95**
Everything® Songwriting Book

## NEW AGE

Everything® Astrology Book, 2nd Ed.
Everything® Birthday Personology Book
**Everything® Celtic Wisdom Book, $15.95**
Everything® Dreams Book, 2nd Ed.
**Everything® Law of Attraction Book, $15.95**
Everything® Love Signs Book, $9.95
Everything® Love Spells Book, $9.95
Everything® Palmistry Book
Everything® Psychic Book
Everything® Reiki Book

Everything® Sex Signs Book, $9.95
Everything® Spells & Charms Book, 2nd Ed.
Everything® Tarot Book, 2nd Ed.
Everything® Toltec Wisdom Book
Everything® Wicca & Witchcraft Book, 2nd Ed.

## PARENTING

Everything® Baby Names Book, 2nd Ed.
Everything® Baby Shower Book, 2nd Ed.
Everything® Baby Sign Language Book with DVD
Everything® Baby's First Year Book
Everything® Birthing Book
Everything® Breastfeeding Book
Everything® Father-to-Be Book
Everything® Father's First Year Book
Everything® Get Ready for Baby Book, 2nd Ed.
Everything® Get Your Baby to Sleep Book, $9.95
Everything® Getting Pregnant Book
Everything® Guide to Pregnancy Over 35
Everything® Guide to Raising a One-Year-Old
Everything® Guide to Raising a Two-Year-Old
Everything® Guide to Raising Adolescent Boys
Everything® Guide to Raising Adolescent Girls
Everything® Mother's First Year Book
Everything® Parent's Guide to Childhood Illnesses
Everything® Parent's Guide to Children and Divorce
Everything® Parent's Guide to Children with ADD/ADHD
Everything® Parent's Guide to Children with Asperger's
    Syndrome
**Everything® Parent's Guide to Children with Anxiety**
Everything® Parent's Guide to Children with Asthma
Everything® Parent's Guide to Children with Autism
Everything® Parent's Guide to Children with Bipolar Disorder
Everything® Parent's Guide to Children with Depression
Everything® Parent's Guide to Children with Dyslexia
Everything® Parent's Guide to Children with Juvenile Diabetes
**Everything® Parent's Guide to Children with OCD**
Everything® Parent's Guide to Positive Discipline
Everything® Parent's Guide to Raising Boys
Everything® Parent's Guide to Raising Girls
Everything® Parent's Guide to Raising Siblings
**Everything® Parent's Guide to Raising Your
    Adopted Child**
Everything® Parent's Guide to Sensory Integration Disorder
Everything® Parent's Guide to Tantrums
Everything® Parent's Guide to the Strong-Willed Child
Everything® Parenting a Teenager Book
Everything® Potty Training Book, $9.95
Everything® Pregnancy Book, 3rd Ed.
Everything® Pregnancy Fitness Book
Everything® Pregnancy Nutrition Book
Everything® Pregnancy Organizer, 2nd Ed., $16.95
Everything® Toddler Activities Book
Everything® Toddler Book
Everything® Tween Book
Everything® Twins, Triplets, and More Book

## PETS

Everything® Aquarium Book
Everything® Boxer Book
Everything® Cat Book, 2nd Ed.
Everything® Chihuahua Book
Everything® Cooking for Dogs Book
Everything® Dachshund Book
Everything® Dog Book, 2nd Ed.
Everything® Dog Grooming Book

Everything® Dog Obedience Book
Everything® Dog Owner's Organizer, $16.95
Everything® Dog Training and Tricks Book
Everything® German Shepherd Book
Everything® Golden Retriever Book
**Everything® Horse Book, 2nd Ed., $15.95**
Everything® Horse Care Book
Everything® Horseback Riding Book
Everything® Labrador Retriever Book
Everything® Poodle Book
Everything® Pug Book
Everything® Puppy Book
Everything® Small Dogs Book
Everything® Tropical Fish Book
Everything® Yorkshire Terrier Book

## REFERENCE

Everything® American Presidents Book
Everything® Blogging Book
Everything® Build Your Vocabulary Book, $9.95
Everything® Car Care Book
Everything® Classical Mythology Book
Everything® Da Vinci Book
Everything® Einstein Book
Everything® Enneagram Book
Everything® Etiquette Book, 2nd Ed.
**Everything® Family Christmas Book, $15.95**
Everything® Guide to C. S. Lewis & Narnia
**Everything® Guide to Divorce, 2nd Ed., $15.95**
Everything® Guide to Edgar Allan Poe
Everything® Guide to Understanding Philosophy
Everything® Inventions and Patents Book
Everything® Jacqueline Kennedy Onassis Book
Everything® John F. Kennedy Book
Everything® Mafia Book
Everything® Martin Luther King Jr. Book
Everything® Pirates Book
Everything® Private Investigation Book
Everything® Psychology Book
Everything® Public Speaking Book, $9.95
Everything® Shakespeare Book, 2nd Ed.

## RELIGION

Everything® Angels Book
Everything® Bible Book
Everything® Bible Study Book with CD, $19.95
Everything® Buddhism Book
Everything® Catholicism Book
Everything® Christianity Book
Everything® Gnostic Gospels Book
**Everything® Hinduism Book, $15.95**
Everything® History of the Bible Book
Everything® Jesus Book
Everything® Jewish History & Heritage Book
Everything® Judaism Book
Everything® Kabbalah Book
Everything® Koran Book
Everything® Mary Book
Everything® Mary Magdalene Book
Everything® Prayer Book

Everything® Saints Book, 2nd Ed.
Everything® Torah Book
Everything® Understanding Islam Book
Everything® Women of the Bible Book
Everything® World's Religions Book

## SCHOOL & CAREERS

Everything® Career Tests Book
Everything® College Major Test Book
Everything® College Survival Book, 2nd Ed.
Everything® Cover Letter Book, 2nd Ed.
Everything® Filmmaking Book
Everything® Get-a-Job Book, 2nd Ed.
Everything® Guide to Being a Paralegal
Everything® Guide to Being a Personal Trainer
Everything® Guide to Being a Real Estate Agent
Everything® Guide to Being a Sales Rep
Everything® Guide to Being an Event Planner
Everything® Guide to Careers in Health Care
Everything® Guide to Careers in Law Enforcement
Everything® Guide to Government Jobs
Everything® Guide to Starting and Running a Catering
  Business
Everything® Guide to Starting and Running a Restaurant
**Everything® Guide to Starting and Running
  a Retail Store**
Everything® Job Interview Book, 2nd Ed.
Everything® New Nurse Book
Everything® New Teacher Book
Everything® Paying for College Book
Everything® Practice Interview Book
Everything® Resume Book, 3rd Ed.
Everything® Study Book

## SELF-HELP

Everything® Body Language Book
Everything® Dating Book, 2nd Ed.
Everything® Great Sex Book
**Everything® Guide to Caring for Aging Parents,
  $15.95**
Everything® Self-Esteem Book
**Everything® Self-Hypnosis Book, $9.95**
Everything® Tantric Sex Book

## SPORTS & FITNESS

Everything® Easy Fitness Book
Everything® Fishing Book
**Everything® Guide to Weight Training, $15.95**
Everything® Krav Maga for Fitness Book
Everything® Running Book, 2nd Ed.
**Everything® Triathlon Training Book, $15.95**

## TRAVEL

Everything® Family Guide to Coastal Florida
Everything® Family Guide to Cruise Vacations
Everything® Family Guide to Hawaii
Everything® Family Guide to Las Vegas, 2nd Ed.
Everything® Family Guide to Mexico
Everything® Family Guide to New England, 2nd Ed.

Everything® Family Guide to New York City, 3rd Ed.
**Everything® Family Guide to Northern California
  and Lake Tahoe**
Everything® Family Guide to RV Travel & Campgrounds
Everything® Family Guide to the Caribbean
Everything® Family Guide to the Disneyland® Resort, California
  Adventure®, Universal Studios®, and the Anaheim
  Area, 2nd Ed.
Everything® Family Guide to the Walt Disney World Resort®,
  Universal Studios®, and Greater Orlando, 5th Ed.
Everything® Family Guide to Timeshares
Everything® Family Guide to Washington D.C., 2nd Ed.

## WEDDINGS

Everything® Bachelorette Party Book, $9.95
Everything® Bridesmaid Book, $9.95
Everything® Destination Wedding Book
Everything® Father of the Bride Book, $9.95
**Everything® Green Wedding Book, $15.95**
Everything® Groom Book, $9.95
**Everything® Jewish Wedding Book, 2nd Ed., $15.95**
Everything® Mother of the Bride Book, $9.95
Everything® Outdoor Wedding Book
Everything® Wedding Book, 3rd Ed.
Everything® Wedding Checklist, $9.95
Everything® Wedding Etiquette Book, $9.95
Everything® Wedding Organizer, 2nd Ed., $16.95
Everything® Wedding Shower Book, $9.95
**Everything® Wedding Vows Book, 3rd Ed., $9.95**
Everything® Wedding Workout Book
Everything® Weddings on a Budget Book, 2nd Ed., $9.95

## WRITING

Everything® Creative Writing Book
Everything® Get Published Book, 2nd Ed.
Everything® Grammar and Style Book, 2nd Ed.
Everything® Guide to Magazine Writing
Everything® Guide to Writing a Book Proposal
Everything® Guide to Writing a Novel
Everything® Guide to Writing Children's Books
Everything® Guide to Writing Copy
Everything® Guide to Writing Graphic Novels
Everything® Guide to Writing Research Papers
**Everything® Guide to Writing a Romance Novel, $15.95**
Everything® Improve Your Writing Book, 2nd Ed.
Everything® Writing Poetry Book